Butter

IN THE

Well

Linda K Hubalek

Butter
IN THE
Well

A Scandinavian Woman's Tale
of Life on the Prairie

Linda K. Hubalek

Hearth
PUBLISHING
A Division of Multi Business Press
Hillsboro, Kansas

Butter in the Well
© 1992 by Linda K. Hubalek

First Edition
Printed in the United States of America
by Multi Business Press, Hillsboro, KS

Library of Congress Catalog Card Number 92-71812
ISBN 9627947-5-9

Maps courtesy of the Kansas State Historical Society.
Photos courtesy of:
    Rozella Schaeffer, Pages—cover, vi, x, 99, 114.
    Melvina Hoglund, Page—62.
    Lester and Ione Johnson, Pages—90, 122.
    Assaria Lutheran Church, Page—108.
    Smoky Valley Genealogical Society and Library, Page —124.

Cover photo—Kajsa Svensson Runeberg

Although the author has exhaustively researched all sources to ensure the accuracy and completeness of the information contained in this book, she assumes no responsibility for errors, inaccuracies, omissions or any other inconsistency herein.

To Maja Kajsa Svensson Runeberg,
the first homesteader,
and my family,
the current homesteaders

South side of house

East side of house, circa 1910.

Acknowledgements

A community of people helped to build this book. Many contributed memories, documents and photographs. Special thanks to Martha Swenson, Rozella Schaeffer, Melvina Hoglund, Ruby Johnson, Alice Larson, Nancy Olsson, Laurina Redden and the relatives and neighbors of the people mentioned in this book.

Thank you to the staffs at the Assaria Lutheran Church, the Salemsborg Lutheran Church, the Kansas State Historical Society, the Smoky Valley Genealogical Society and Library, the Campbell Room of Kansas in the Salina Library, the Folklife Institute of Central Kansas and the Family History Center of The Church of Jesus Christ of Later-day Saints.

I wish to express special gratitude to my research assistants, Lester and Ione Johnson and Leland Akers, my editor, Alice Sky, and my special adviser, Verne Hubalek.

Tack så mycket.

Linda K. Hubalek

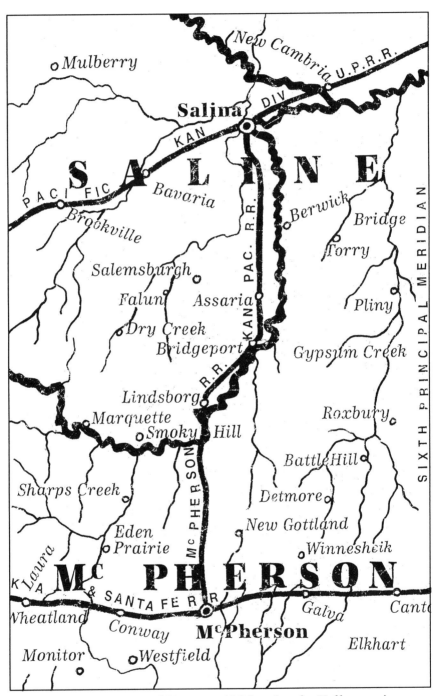

Gray's New Map of Kansas, 1881—Smoky Valley region

Table of Contents

*Standing: Christina, Alfred, Willie, Julia, Carrie and Alma.
Seated: Second husband Peter, Mabel and Kajsa.*

Preface

This book is about a Swedish emigrant woman who homesteaded Kansas land in 1868. Maja Kajsa Svensson was a young bride of one year when she, her husband, Carl Johan, and 3-month-old daughter, Anna Christina, left Sweden in 1867.

Born to Johan Magnus Andersson and Anna Lisa Mattesdotter on June 15, 1844, in Klevmarken, Sweden, she was the first in her family to marry and the first to move to America.

After receiving an encouraging letter from a friend who had moved and settled in Illinois, the Svenssons set sail for America and settled in Jacksonville, Illinois. Carl worked in his friend's brickyard but dreamed of farming his own land. The farmland in Illinois had already been bought up, so they needed to look elsewhere. Land agents canvassing Illinois advertised the free land in Kansas, just waiting to be claimed. Although Kajsa would have preferred to stay in Illinois, she accepted Carl's decision and packed for the trip to Kansas.

This fictionalized account describes Kajsa's first 20 years on her Kansas farm and how the community developed into the Smoky Valley region of Saline County, Kansas. It is seen through her eyes, as though she were writing in her journal.

I interviewed relatives and neighbors who remember stories of this family and the history of this area. I walked the cemeteries to find the tombstones of Kajsa's relatives. Some stories, dates and name spellings have conflicted at times, but I have tried to find the truth by researching church, cemetery and county records. Old newspapers and books have shed light on the conditions and events that took place in the communities.

The accounts of Kajsa are meant to portray life during the late 1800s in the Smoky Valley of Kansas. Some license has been taken to depict the everyday events in the life of a family in this time period.

I have not found pictures of her family prior to 1881, but those of the family and farm in later years reveal much about Kajsa's life.

Kajsa's daughter Julia married Peter Olson's son Joseph, and spent her married life on his family farm directly north of where she was born. "Aunt Julia," as almost everyone in the neighborhood called her, was like a grandmother to me. I used to take her a May Day basket filled with lilac blooms picked from the bush she helped her mother plant.

But just as important as knowing Kajsa's family, I know the farm they homesteaded, for I grew up on that very land, roamed its acres and lived in the house that Carl and Kajsa built. Living on the land has given me a depth and feel for the life of the woman portrayed in these pages.

In Kajsa's photos, she stares me straight in the eye as if challenging me to look into her soul. Kajsa looked like a quiet, determined woman who loved her family and land. Her story ought to be told.

Introduction

Life in Sweden in the 1800s was very hard for the common people. It was the custom to divide the family farm among the sons when they were of age and many farms had been divided too often over time. Because of this, there was not enough good land to support growing families. Most of the farmland was rocky and hilly as well, and crop failures, followed by famine, plagued the people. The social class system of the country prevented the farmer from getting ahead. He was obliged to be subservient to the king, the sheriff and the church warden, and to pay high taxes. People were not able to worship as they chose and this caused discontent.

When travel by ship became possible to the new world in North America, this offered an escape for vast numbers of Swedes. The people who had forged ahead sent back glowing accounts of the richness of the land, freedom of religion and equality among all of the people. In 1862, the Homestead Act was passed giving settlers land to live on and cultivate.

Sweden's farmers started to think about moving when their crops failed and their children were starving. America seemed to be the land of hope and salvation.

Families sold what little they had to buy passage to the new country, and often arrived with only a trunk of belongings. They left behind the familiar for a land where they didn't know the culture, language or people. Parents left behind in Sweden would rarely see their sons, daughters or grandchildren again. And most of these New World emigrants would never again set foot on Sweden's soil.

The courage and strength it took for families to strike out on their own was phenomenal. With only the strength of their backs and the sweat of their brows they turned native prairie land into self-sufficient farms. In the earliest days of homesteading, the few new towns were often far away. There was little money to buy supplies or food, so they had to make do with what was available on the land. Neighbors might be miles away, which made life on the farm a world of its own. Husband and wife were totally dependent on each other for food, shelter and support.

Extremely cold winters and hot humid summers made life miserable in the crude early shelters in which many emigrant families and their animals lived. Crop failures, disease and death were common the first few years. Only perseverance and faith in God kept the people alive, sane and forging on. The picture may seem grim, but that was the life of the homesteader.

Life on the farm usually got better as the years went by. After the farmers had broken enough acres, they often sold their extra crops for cash and bought lumber and tools to improve their homes and barns.

Almost all of the land available in the Smoky Valley region was homesteaded or bought by the late 1870s. Soon neighborhoods of farms sprung up, followed by trading centers, churches and schools.

Whenever possible, money was sent back to Sweden so parents and other relatives could come to the new country.

The land along the Smoky Hill River was settled mostly by Swedes. Farms flourished and were passed on to future generations. Today, more than 100 years later, the influence of these pioneers can still be seen and felt.

Go back to a time when there are no streets, roads or cars. Imagine there are no buildings, homes, hospitals or grocery stores around the corner. All of your family's belonging fit in a small wooden wagon. The year is 1868. There is nothing but tall, green waving grass as far as the eye can see. The scent of warm spring air after a morning rain surrounds you. Spring blows gently in your face. The snort of the horse and an occasional meadowlark, whistling its call, are the only sounds. You are alone on the virgin land of the vast prairie.

1868

Our Own Land

March 7

Ellsworth, Kansas —I want to keep a journal of our adventure into the American Plains so I will have an account of what our first years were like.

In spring of '67 we traveled from Klevmarken, Sweden, to New York City, America, by ship, then by train to Jacksonville, Illinois. Now a year later, we're back on a train heading for the open prairies of Kansas.

We traveled from Jacksonville to St. Louis first. In Illinois we saw meadows of grass, wooded areas and towns. The scenery was much the same until we got past Kansas City. Then there were very few trees and the prairie grass stretched as far as the eye could see. The few towns we've gone through were very small and new. The farther west, the sparser it has gotten. I've heard Kansas called "the Great American Desert," but everything looks green. Of course it's spring now. Maybe the whole countryside dries up in the summer.

We were to get off at the town of Salina, in Saline County. Our friends in Jacksonville put destination tags on us and our belongings since we don't know much of the American language yet. Most people in Jacksonville were Swedish, so we got along fine. Carl knows a few American words, since he had to work and did the shopping when we lived there.

The ride has been wearing on us. This morning Carl looked like he didn't feel good. The motion of the train car bouncing on the track and smoke from the engine's smokestack has made us all a little sick.

I was trying to watch the railroad station signs at each stop, but they were not always in sight. Each time Carl tried to find the conductor, to see if that was the place we were to get off. Instead of trying to ask, it was easier to point to his name tag.

At the last stop Carl rushed up to me and said: "Gather up our things and Christina! We've got to get off. This is Ellsworth. We missed Salina!"

I panicked when I realized we missed our stop. But, I knew Carl would figure out a way to get us back on the track to our destination. We have found overnight lodging and we will travel back to Salina tomorrow.

This was be an extra expense we didn't need.

March 30

Carl came down with the fever and chills of ague that night here in Ellsworth. Thank the Lord he is finally getting over it. It could have been worse. I could have become a widow with a 15-month-old baby in a strange American town.

We've been at the Railroad Hotel for over three weeks. I've had to help the cook prepare and serve the meals in exchange for room and board for our small family. We were lucky to find a innkeeper so kind.

Tomorrow we'll get back on the train heading for Salina. This time we will get off at the right town.

March 31

By the creek on our land —When we arrived in Salina today, we bought a wagon, an ox, a horse, lumber for the buildings, a 100-pound sack of flour and a few supplies. We spent practically all of our money in one day. There wasn't much selection in the little town of Salina. It was just a handful of shanties and a few businesses. I was expecting an established town like Jacksonville.

The storekeeper pointed out a land agent's office where the man understood Swedish. We wanted to homestead along the Smoky Hill River, but the agent said the lands south of Salina and west of the river have been bought up by land companies or granted to the railroad. He showed us a map of the county and Carl picked out land east of the river on Section 30, Township 16 South, Range 2 West. It has a creek running through it and the river nearby.

When we left Salina, we traveled to the southeast for almost 16 miles. We know about how many minutes it takes a wagon to go a mile, so we knew when we got close to our land. The agent kept looking to the west to keep the river in view. It was a good thing he was on a tall horse since the grass is 5 feet high. He was looking for the cornerstone that was put in place when the land was surveyed. He had the survey notes and plat map with him, but they were not very accurate so it took a while to find our boundaries.

I couldn't believe how much land is in 80 acres. No one in our parish in Sweden had this much land to himself.

The creek does not have a whole lot of water in it, but it is moving and clear. We have water to drink for ourselves and our animals. I was disappointed when the land agent said our creek will be dry by the end of summer. We'll have to dig a well before the water stops running.

When I need to wash clothes, I'll do it right on the creek bank. I can spread the clothes out to dry on the bushes that are growing in clusters nearby. The taller ones are a cloud of clear white blossoms. I believe they're plums. How about that, we already have fruit trees on our property. The shorter bush with the knobby bark and yellow teardrop flower reminds me of the gooseberry plant my neighbor had in her yard in Illinois. The fruit made wonderful pies and jellies.

Our land seems to slope down to the west toward the creek, then rises again abruptly. There are just a few trees—"cottonwood," I believe they are called—right on the west side of the bank. These are the only trees on our land.

The trees of the Smoky Hill River loom up within a half mile west of our homestead. No one lives in that area yet, so we will be free to hunt and fish along its banks.

We like the northeast land the best for our home and buildings. We're close to the creek and the place where four parcels of land meet. Hopefully other settlers will homestead the other three corners and we will have neighbors nearby.

Tonight and for quite a while we will sleep in the wagon and cook on the campfire. We stacked the lumber beside the wagon, so we have more room in the wagon bed. Carl may sleep on the ground, but Christina needs to be protected from the damp ground and the creatures that I'm sure will check us out tonight.

3

Thank goodness Christina has stayed healthy. Many children died on the long trip to America and were buried at sea. It broke my heart to hear about parents burying their babies along the wagon trails going west. The families had to move on, knowing they would never visit the grave. One woman told me she hoped her little one would be left in peace and not dug up by a wolf looking for food, or an Indian looking for clothing.

My thoughts have been interrupted several times by the dark clouds building up above the bluffs to the west. We experienced a few thunderstorms in Illinois and Christina was terrified. I was pretty uneasy myself. We were in a house then, not out in the wide open, lost in a sea of waving grass.

The wind has picked up. In the distance the clouds seem to be gaining size and speed, and heading toward us. The sky is growing much too dark for this time of day. Carl has walked down to the creek with a wooden bucket to fetch our water and to gather fuel for a fire.

Our basket of bread and salted meat that I packed in Ellsworth will last us awhile. I can see I'm going to have to be very creative in cooking this year until our first crops come in.

My mind today has been a constant jumble of questions. Does Carl know what he's getting us into? Will we survive by ourselves in the middle of nowhere?

Oh Lord God, please look after my family. Ease my mind. I wish we would have passed a farmstead so we knew we had some neighbors.

It's beginning to rain. I hope the wagon sheet covering our belongings does not leak. The rumbling in the distance keeps echoing closer and closer to our little camp. That crack of lightning was too close. Where is Carl?!

April 1

It poured all last night, maybe a slight pause, and then more buckets of rain. Carl and I were soaking wet, trying to keep Christina and our supplies halfway dry. Our poor animals were tied to the wagon, having no choice but to be miserable where they stood.

In the dawn light we saw we were surrounded by water. The creek had flooded its banks and was rising around us. Our stack of boards was floating away so Carl and I had to jump from the wagon and splash around in the muddy waters, shoving the lumber back into the wagon. We had to move farther up our land to the northeast to escape the floodwater. The creek I was so happy about had become a life-threatening curse. It is evening now and the water is receding. We now know that the land will be our master and not the other way around.

April 8

I'm so hot and sweaty today. But I need my long-sleeved dress to protect me from the sun's burning rays and the insects. We've been digging on the well for days. Carl fills the bucket up with dirt from the bottom of the hole, then I pull it up by a rope, dump the bucket and send it back down to him. He is very discouraged. First we almost get flooded out by the creek, and now we can't find any water.

April 9

"I give up," Carl said as he slumped at the bottom of the hole. "There's no water here. We're going to have to move to a different site."

We're both tired, sunburned and disillusioned with our first week on our land. Tonight Carl took a walk to the river and shot a turkey for our supper. He needed a walk to cool down and I needing time to sit and rest my weary back and arms. We have so much digging ahead. I'm going to have to get used to doing hard physical work again. Life in Jacksonville softened my body.

Christina is getting tired of being in the wagon but that's the way it will have to be. If she wanders away in this tall grass, we could lose her forever.

April 15

The creek runs through our land, across the south and up the west side until it empties into the river on the next section to the north of us. We moved our little camp into the middle of our farm on the far east edge since we know the creek can surprise us with a flood. Again we started the process of digging the well, one scoop at a time. Today we were rewarded with water.

April 18

Today we start digging our home. I hate to live in the ground, burrowed in like a gopher, but we can't afford the lumber it takes to build a house. What lumber we did find money for will be used sparingly.

People say being in the ground protects you from the heat of the summer day and the freezing cold of winter. It will only be about 10 by 12 feet in size, just enough for our bodies and belongings. I'll continue to cook outside on an open fire. We've scoured the creek for rocks to reinforce our walls. For our dugout to be a legal homestead house, we must have one window in it. We bought a small pane of glass in Salina that Carl will frame and put next to the door.

April 23

Carl left ledges along the inside walls of the dugout to use for sitting and sleeping. He dug two additional recesses, one for a safe spot to sit a candle and another to hide our food away from the vermin.

We cut strips of sod, about 12 by 18 by 2 inches, and laid them around the edge of our hole to build walls 3 feet high. This will give us the extra height to stand the door upright on the south end. Carl chopped down one tall straight tree by the river for the ridgepole. Fallen timber from the river and a few boards make up the roof rafters that were to nailed the ridgepole. We had a wagonload of tree limbs that we weaved in among the rafters. Next, dry grass, from around the house was layered on, then sod blocks on the roof. We threw dirt back on the roof from the hole that was dug. Just another day or two and we'll move in.

April 25

We saved the hard layer of sand from when we dug the well. This sand, and clay from the river bank, were mixed with water to plaster the walls of the dugout. It's very crude, but it will have to do for our first winter. The dirt floor will get packed down in time. I'll sprinkle my dishwater on it to help it harden. I wish we had rugs to cover the floor. It would make it warmer and easier to keep clean. I talked Carl into cutting up one board for a door. At least I'll feel a little safer at night with it closed. The hungry howling of the wolves scares me.

April 28

Our sparse belongings from the wagon have filled the dugout in a hurry. Carl made two chairs out of a log he sawed up. Another board was fashioned into a table. The crate that held our supplies will be my cupboard. A lean-to bed is braced on the right side of the dugout, half on the ledge for support. Christina's cradle fits under our bed when the cradle is not being used. A crude mattress was fashioned out of ticking filled with "prairie feathers." I'm glad we brought along the bedding from our house in Jacksonville.

Carl found some old buffalo horns when he was out walking. He nailed them up to the wall to hang our clothes on.

April 29

We hung the wagon sheet up as our ceiling for the dugout today. Last night there was a rattlesnake dangling from the rafters above Christina! Lord give me strength. I cannot get used to those things. Fear runs down my spine every time I see one. I'm tired of the snakes, mice and insects that drop down on us by surprise during a meal or during the night. Now that the weather has warmed up, the snakes are everywhere. I'm petrified one of us will get bitten and die on the spot. We were down at the creek yesterday for a few hours and came home to six vipers sunning themselves on the south side of the dugout. We've trampled down the grass around our "home," but it does not seem to deter the snakes. I must carry a big stick wherever I go, so I can beat them out of our path. I can't let Christina out of my sight now that she's starting to walk.

We also have at least one pack rat that is stealing everything that I leave out. If I ever see it, I'm going to shoot it. I am almost as good a shot as Carl and I won't hesitate at the trigger for the rat that stole my thimble.

May 1

I'm ready to move back to Illinois, or back to Sweden. Besides the three of us in bed, we have the company of a multitude of bedbugs that have hatched out of my "prairie feather" mattress. Fleas jump all over the floor (we have no dog to blame), a toad somewhere in the sod roof croaks all night, and crickets, spiders and mosquitoes are everywhere. Carl keeps telling me that conditions will get better in time.

May 2

We had rain last night, outside and some inside. Globs of mud and water fell through the roof where the wagon sheet was not covering the ceiling. The sheet was starting to fill up and bow from the weight of the mud, so we had to lift it up in the middle and let the watery mess drain down the walls. Two snakes and *the toad* slid down too. I hope this first rain will seal the roof so it does not keep leaking every time.

May 8

Although the sun has been out for days, the ceiling is still leaking from the rain we got earlier this week. It stays a fairly comfortable temperature and damp inside, but outside it is hot and steamy.

It's too muddy to start working the ground for our first field, but conditions are good to cut sod for a lean-to shelter for the animals. We dug a base for the shed and Carl cut some straight saplings for the four corner posts. It will be open to the south and provide a basic shelter from the weather. Tree limbs will be laid across the ridgepoles and prairie grass, sod blocks and dirt laid on top, much like the house. In time we'll need to build a barn for the animals and a crib for the harvest storage. There is so much to do, but no money to do it with. We took the farm buildings in Sweden for granted.

I'm getting good at cooking over a campfire, but I miss my oven for baking bread. We're eating a lot of beans, corn mush and biscuits that I make in the skillet. There is plenty of wild game in the area. Prairie chickens and rabbits have been our main food source. Carl has seen a herd of deer by the river, but we have no way to preserve the meat yet so we'll wait until fall.

I found a nest of prairie chicken eggs today. It was a treat to have fried eggs for a change. I'm hungry for vegetables but we don't have a garden yet. I need a space cleared for the garden, and Carl needs to plant at least an acre of corn as soon as possible. Since we don't have a plow yet to break the sod into a field, we'll cut the grass, poke holes in the ground and throw the seed in. By autumn, we must have an area ready for wheat planting.

May 9

We have neighbors! Carl met Benjamin Robinson while he was hunting along the river today. Benjamin had heard gunshots becoming regular in the area so he decided to investigate.

Benjamin and his wife, Adelaide, live one mile north and a quarter mile east of us. They are English people who came from

Mount Vernon, Maine, to Junction City, Kansas, in '59, then to Saline County in '60. I asked if they had any children. Carl said they lost an infant son last September, but Adelaide is expecting a child later this year.

Benjamin bought land beside his homestead land and needs help this summer to harvest his crops. In exchange for Carl's labor, we will use his plow to break our sod and he'll give us seed wheat, Indian corn and potato eyes to get our own fields started.

May 11

This morning we drove our wagon to the Robinsons' to get the plow. Although they are not Swedish it was good to meet them. Adelaide was as happy to see another woman in the area as I was. We will have to work on the language barrier so we can visit.

Fresh milk from their cow was a real treat for all of us today. I hope Carl can eventually buy a heifer calf from the Robinsons so we can have milk every day for drinking and cooking. In Sweden, the women and girls take care of the cows and milk them. That is one chore that I have missed since we moved to America.

She has a flock of chickens. Adelaide promised me a setting hen and some eggs later in the spring when we have a place for them.

Adelaide gave me a loaf of rye bread, still warm from the oven, to take home with us. We ate half of it before we got back to the dugout.

We are lucky to have such close neighbors that are willing to give us a hand. God is looking out for us in our new land.

May 15

Carl went to Salina today for supplies, so he dropped us off at the Robinsons' for the day. I think he noticed I was getting depressed and needed someone to talk to.

Benjamin has a black man, Larry Lapsley, working for him. The Robinsons have taken him under their wing and helped him quite a bit. Adelaide is teaching him to read and write. During dinner he told me about how he happened to be living in Kansas. He is an interesting fellow, full of stories.

Larry was a slave who escaped from his owner and traveled by foot from Texas to freedom in Kansas.

He was born in Danville, Kentucky, in March of '40, to slaves on the Lapsley plantation. I believe he and his family were treated well, as he has good memories of the lady of the plantation. Larry remembers Widow Lapsley on her death bed, saying to her son Samuel, "Keep my boy (meaning Larry, her slave), as long as you live, to remember me by."

Two years later when Samuel Lapsley had gone through his inheritance, he moved to Jackson County, Missouri. He bought 80 acres of land, farmed it for three years, then sold it and bought a livery stable in Pleasant Hill, Missouri. Larry, his mother and two of his cousins moved with their master Samuel.

Samuel Lapsley was heavy in debt so he decided to sell Larry to his brother-in law, William Bunor. When the Union Army moved into Missouri during the Civil War, many slave holders fled to Texas. In December of '61, Larry moved to Bonham, Texas, driving a wagonload of women and children slaves for his new master.

Mr. Bunor hired Larry out to a whiskey distillery where he worked for three years. After that, Larry was to be sold to a man he didn't want to work for. When the time came to move, Larry and his cousin Tom ran away, heading north to the Union lines where they could be free.

Larry said they traveled only at night, staying off the roads. Because of heavy rains that slowed their pace and confused their sense of direction, they covered only a few miles the first three days. Tom talked Larry into traveling in the early morning so they could see where they were going, but this led to capture by some Southern-sympathizing Indians.

Tom and Larry were the Indians' slaves for four weeks. They were chained together the first two weeks, with a guard watching them all the time. Eventually their captors took the chains off their wrists and let them have separate leg chains during the day to work. At night they were chained back together.

Larry said he decided the only way he was going to escape was to gain the Indians' confidence by cooperating with them. He was able to hide a hatchet near the cabin when he was working outside.

One night, as the Indians were having an important dance ceremony, there was a terrible rainstorm. Larry told the guard he had to step outside a minute to relieve himself. Once outside, Larry found the hatchet, pried the lock off his leg chains and ran off into the stormy night.

He spent five days, without food or sleep, hiding from the Indians and their hunting dogs. He stood for two days, neck deep in river water under the cover of an overhanging willow tree. He didn't have anything to eat except some corn in his pocket that actually sprouted since he had been wet for so many days.

After the Indians gave up their search for him, he walked north until he came to a deserted Indian village with wild hogs and cattle nearby. Union soldiers had used this area the winter before, and there was a large building with papers and tools left behind. Completely worn out and starving, he cornered a hog in the old smokehouse and clubbed it to death with an ax. He found three matches in the building. Two were bad, but the last one started a fire and Larry roasted his pig.

After 12 days, he finally had the strength to move on. He continued north, where he met friendly Creek Indians who fed him and took him to Fort Gibson in Cherokee Nation.

Larry had traveled almost 200 miles on foot to safety. At the fort, Col. Luke Parsons gave him clothing and medicine, and hired him to take care of his two horses for 10 dollars a month plus room and board.

After being mustered out of the war, Col. Parsons brought Larry to Kansas, where the colonel owned a house. I believe he said they arrived in Salina in July of '65. The Smoky Hill River was so high they had to wait on the east side for three weeks before they chanced swimming across.

Larry worked for Col. Parsons for 13 months before he came to live and work with Benjamin.

I have a hard enough time understanding English, let alone Larry's southern accent, but he is patient with my Swedish and we converse in an awkward way. Larry seems genuinely interested in our family and our homeland.

I showed Adelaide the rashes on our arms, telling her that they itch so bad. She says it's the "Kansas Itch" that newcomers get and there's not much we can do about it. It will fade in time. Christina and I are getting so sunburnt. Our pale Swedish skin is not used to being in the sun most of the day. Adelaide gave me one of her sunbonnets to wear. It looks hot and tends to make me look like a horse with blinders on, but I'm sure it will help. I need to fashion a small one for Christina out of scrap material. I have some left from when I cut up one of my petticoats for a curtain on my pantry box.

I feel so much better after spending the day with my neighbor.

May 19

We've had mellow weather and soft winds this week. Carl got the sod broken for the garden north of the house. It felt so good to have the warm brown earth beneath my toes. Christina toddled around, picking up clods and earthworms while I hoed rows and planted the seeds. I planted the two bushels of potato eyes I cut up yesterday. In exchange for Carl's work at the Robinsons' we got the potatoes, corn and vegetable seeds. If everything grows, we'll have pumpkins, squash, carrots, beans and the potatoes to store for our winter supply. I can't wait for the vegetables to grow so we can have something fresh to eat.

May 25

We got the corn planted. Now we pray that the rains come at the right time so we get a good stand. We need corn for the horse and for our cornmeal. We are so dependent on our land this year.

Carl saw three Kaw Indians near the river today. They haven't bothered us yet and I hope they keep their distance.

June 10

The prairie is blooming. With the rains and warm temperatures have come flowers hidden in the grass. I don't know what they are, but it softens my heart to see pink, yellow and white flowers dotting the landscape as I roam our land looking for buffalo chips. It's hard to carry Christina, my snake club and the sack of chips too. I fashioned our gunny sack into an apron. At least the chips are light in weight. I think I'll gather flower seeds this fall and scatter them on top of the sod roof of the dugout so we'll have a flower bed on top of the house next spring.

June 15

My 24th birthday —The days are getting hotter. Very early in the morning, we wake to the song of the meadowlark. We just have ground birds since there are no trees nearby. I try to get the outside chores done first thing in the morning so we can spend the midday inside the dugout where we are protected from the heat and sun.

Some days are so still and sticky that you feel like you are going to suffocate. But other days the wind is blowing so hot and hard you feel like you are standing in front of a blazing fire. When the wind is blowing like that it is hard to stand or walk. You have to lean into it to keep from blowing over. I get so exhausted from fighting the wind. Christina has to hold my hand to keep from being swept away.

The garden seedlings are up, but I'm afraid the wind will blow the plants out of the ground. In the evening I have been drawing water from the well and giving the tomato and vine plants a drink. I hunger for a tomato so bad I can't let the plants die.

June 24

Midsummer's Day is on my mind today. In Sweden my family will have decorated the house with birch branches, and *Moder* will have made her mouth-watering pastries for visitors. They will go to a church service to celebrate the start of summer. I was feeling blue, so I cut some cottonwood branches from a tree down by the river and draped them over the dugout door to remind me of the birch trees back home. I don't know if that helped or made me feel worse. I told Christina all the stories I could think of about the holiday. Of course she is too small to understand, but it helped me reminisce. Carl is working at the Robinsons' today, so I am alone with her again.

June 26

We have seen quite a few buffalo this year. In fact, two ended up as buffalo robes for us to use this winter. The meat is strong-tasting and stringy, but it makes good stew. Mr. Lapsley had been to Salina and was told that a herd 30 miles long was seen 10 miles south of us. When the herd got to the Smoky Hill River, it almost drank the river dry.

June 29

Went down to the river and picked mulberries early this morning. I only found one tree and it is not very old, but it had berries on it. I don't know what was more stained from the purple juice, my hands, the apron that I gathered them in, or Christina's face after she ate so many. I'm going to make a mulberry pie and dry the rest of the fruit for winter.

I saw a swarm of bees around the old hollow tree across the way. I hope I can get some honey from it this fall since I don't have any sugar for sweetener. Nearby was a grapevine with clusters of green grapes. We'll see if I or the wild animals get them first when they turn purple.

July 1

I've gotten used to the heat, but today I swear it was over 100 degrees. I picked three bushels of wild plums from the thicket on the creek. Christina sat in the wagon jabbering to the ox. The bees and flies buzzed around my head as I pushed through the thicket. I scratched up my face in the process and tore a hole in my dress sleeve. Some of the plums had worms in them, but I'll dry them anyway.

July 20

I had a scare today while washing clothes. The fire pit is deep and lined with rock, but I still have to be very careful in case the wind is blowing. A gust came out of nowhere and blew a spark into the grass. I had been stirring the pot of clothes with a stick. I reacted so fast I threw out half the clothes as I flung the stick around to beat the spark out. Christina was sitting nearby. I could have scalded her to death and started a prairie fire all at the same time. Carl was working at the Robinsons' today, so I was on my own.

Tonight when we said our evening prayers I gave my deepest thanks to the Lord for watching over us today.

July 29

It has been a long, hot month, dry and windy, with no rain for three weeks. Carl goes to the Robinsons' almost every morning to hoe the weeds out of the fields. I've been pulling weeds from our own cornfield and the garden. Killed five snakes today. They were seeking shade in my squash vines.

We have been living on fresh tomatoes and corn. It feels good to sink my teeth in a red ripe tomato and let the juice run down my chin!

August 6

Windy today. We smelled smoke this afternoon but couldn't see any fire. Sod roofs are supposed to be fireproof, but I don't want to find out. We have so very little to our name, I would hate to lose anything.

I don't know if I could outrun a prairie fire, but I would grab Christina, jump on the horse and try. Depending on which direction the fire was coming from, I would try to get to the river. We would stay in the water until the fire jumped the river and moved on. Carl walks to Robinsons' so I have the horse at home with me. When he goes to town, he walks or takes the ox and wagon. Carl carved a box to keep our homestead papers in. I could put that in my gunny sack apron with our Bible and other cherished things and take them with us.

It's late, and as we sit here the sky has the telltale glow of an approaching fire. I wonder if it will reach us. We'll have to stay alert tonight.

Wait, the wind is dying down; it's starting to rain. That will take care of the fire.

August 7

Since it was a calm morning, I made biscuits. It is too dangerous to start a campfire when it is windy. I made enough to last us several days in case it gets windy again. I'm just mixing flour, water and salt for the stiff dough, then cooking them on my skillet.

We haven't had meat for days because of the wind. I can't cook up meat ahead because it spoils so fast. The dugout has been too warm this month to keep meat. I hope we have enough vegetables so Carl can trade them in Salina for some rope and crocks for me to store food in the well where it is dark and cool.

August 17

Carl has borrowed the plow this week to turn sod for our fall wheat. He hopes to get five acres ready. It takes five bushels of wheat to grind down to 200 pounds of flour. After we get our first crop, we also need to keep back some for seed wheat for next year.

I am spending most of my time in the garden after I get the household chores done for the day. I have taken a few turns at the plow while Carl is hunting. We hate to let the plow sit idle since we are borrowing it.

September 4

The relentless heat has let go of the earth this month. The evenings are cooling down and we don't see as many snakes.

Started digging potatoes today. We'll let them dry in the field before we store them. We need to dig a pit for winter storage for our produce. We will cover it up with grass and dirt, then uncover it when we need to get something out. I'll keep as much as I can in the dugout, but there isn't much room.

September 15

The dew on the grass has been so thick in the morning that my feet and skirt get soaking wet. Carl has been cutting grass and stacking it in a mound for hay for the animals this winter. We will twist it into braids to use for our winter fire too, if the ground is covered with snow and we can't find enough buffalo chips. We took the ox and wagon to the south the other day and spent most of the day picking up chips. Carl has stacked them in a cone shape so the rainwater runs off. It is right beside the dugout, so I don't have far to go. We hope to get at least 10 wagonloads of chips stacked before we start planting wheat.

September 28

First frost on the garden this morning. The vines were covered with a blanket of furry ice crystals at first sunlight, and by afternoon they were black and limp. Luckily I picked all the tomatoes last night, red and green, guessing that time was running out on the warm weather. I'll fry the green tomatoes. We have to use everything we harvest and make it stretch until next year.

I harvested the pumpkins and squash today, stacked some in the corner of the dugout and put the rest in the storage pit. I think we had a good first crop on the native prairie. Benjamin said this was a dry year compared to the past, but this seems to be fertile ground and produced much more than our land in Sweden would have.

I plan to harvest the beans tomorrow. They are hard and the shells are now dry and brittle. The easiest way to shell the beans will be to put the pods in the gunny sack, stomp on the sack to crush them, then pour them into the wash tub. The wind will blow the broken pod pieces away and let the beans fall into the tub.

October 3

Tonight before it got completely dark, we went down to the river to harvest the honey from the tree I saw when Christina and I picked mulberries. Since it was cold today, and we went at dusk, the bees did not bother us. I'm glad we took the washtub because there was a big honeycomb and it was a sticky mess. Carl and I had honey all over us by the time we got the comb out of the tree hollow. It will be so good to have sweetener for my baking again. I miss not having white sugar.

We have been busy as those bees this month trying to get enough food ready to last the winter. We don't have any hogs or cattle to butcher. Carl has shot several deer and we cut up the venison in small strips to dry. Since we have not been here through a winter, we don't know what the weather will be like or if we will find fresh game to eat. If we get a bad blizzard, where we cannot get out for days, we must have food stashed ahead and ready. I think in some ways we might be naive about this country, but the Robinsons have been a great help to us in that respect.

October 16

We could see our breath on this frosty morning as we rode out to the edge of the corn field. Another day of snapping the corn (with husks left on) from the dry stalks. We have been picking corn for one week. (I am very thankful we observe Sunday as the Lord's day to rest. I needed the break yesterday. Working in the field and trying to keep up on the cooking and housework has been taxing.) After we shell the corn, we will use the husk and cob for fuel. Carl made a temporary sod shed to store the wheat and corn. He hopes to build a granary next year for better storage.

I bundle up Christina and she plays in the wagon with a rolled up sock that she pretends is a doll, or she sleeps while we're working. The ox just stands there until Carl tells it to move forward. We start early in the morning, stop for dinner, then snap corn until sunset. I hope we can get done before the weather turns bad. It is a back-breaking job, but it would be even worse if the stalks fall over. We also planted some broomcorn plants so Carl can make brooms for me. Even though the dugout floor is dirt, it still needs to be swept.

October 29

Laura Adelaide Robinson was born today. I'm so thankful that Adelaide and the baby are all right. Now Christina will have a playmate. Adelaide's sister is staying with them to help for a while.

November 9

When I woke up this morning I couldn't figure out what the white drift on the inside of the door was. I was not awake enough to realize it was snow. We had our first snow last night and it had sifted through the cracks. Christina touched it, then put a little in her mouth. She squealed when she found out it was cold. She was too little last year to remember snow. There was a thin layer of ice in the water bucket in the dugout this morning. It's hard to crawl out of our warm bed to make breakfast outside.

Carl shot a skunk while I was making breakfast. Skunk fat is supposed to be good for healing skin sores. Our hands are so chapped from snapping corn in this cold weather. We will see if it works. The fat is also good for greasing boots to make them waterproof.

We are out of coffee beans. I have been roasting wheat until it is dark brown, then boiling it in water and straining off the "coffee." It is a dark and hot drink, but it is a poor substitute for coffee.

November 26

We celebrated the American holiday called Thanksgiving with the Robinsons today. We were thankful to be asked to their home. They live in a dugout too, but have two rooms and real furniture. Benjamin had shot a turkey down near their bend of the river. He said that turkey is the traditional meat for the Thanksgiving meal back East. But Adelaide also fixed venison, potatoes, creamed hominy corn, pickled beets, fresh wheat bread (I had two thick slices) and dried currant pie. Since she has a cow, we also enjoyed fresh butter and cheese. Adelaide sent home a wedge of cheese and a loaf of bread. She is so thoughtful.

Mr. Lapsley was also there. He told us about the fancy dinners at the Kentucky plantation where he grew up. In some ways I think he misses those days.

Benjamin said there is a pair of Swedes from Jämshög who bought land last month from the National Land Company about 5 miles northwest of us. They paid $3.50 an acre. Both men filed homestead claims for family members too. One man, Bengt Hessler, has two brothers, Sven and Olaf, and a sister, Bothilda, who are coming over in the next year or so. The other man is Bengt's cousin, Måns Peterson. His parents and siblings arrived in Chicago in May. Måns Peterson apparently came on ahead to find land. I was glad to hear that Swedes are moving into the area. We will have people that know our language and celebrate our holidays and customs.

December 7

Christina's second birthday—Our little girl is growing up. She may have been born in Sweden, but she will be an American girl. Besides starting to speak Swedish, she is picking up English words from the Robinsons and Indian words from Mr. Lapsley's Indian stories.

December 9

Since Carl is spending most of his time inside now that it is cold, he has been carving. He has made some wooden spoons and small bowls for me, and tool handles for himself. He carved a doll's head and I added a little body for it out of one of Christina's first dresses. It will be her Christmas present.

Carl bought a two-lidded stove in Salina this month to heat the dugout and so I could do some of my cooking inside. It is a very small second-hand stove, but better than cooking everything outside.

Since the days are shorter and sometimes overcast, we need more light in the dugout. Rather than use up the supply of candles, we are burning a plate of tallow, using a piece of twisted cloth as the wick, or burning the tailfeathers of ducks and geese. I don't care for the smell of singed feathers, but I have to use what we've got.

December 13

At home in Sweden the Christmas season starts today on Saint Lucia's Day. When I was living at home, Sara, my oldest sister, would wake us up early with coffee and cakes in bed. She wore the traditional white robe, crimson sash and a crown of lighted candles that illuminated the dark to represent Saint Lucia, the patron saint of Sweden.

Special food was prepared for the holiday season. *Fader* was in charge of the meats and Moder baked enough pastries for us and anyone who came to visit. The *smörgåsbord* on Christmas Eve was loaded with the traditional Christmas dishes.

Seemed like we had barely gone to bed when it was time to rise and walk to *Julotta*. The rest of the day was spent quietly at home with our family. We would open our gifts, handmade items that everyone had secretly worked on for weeks before Christmas.

I remember the *ljus krona* that sat on the corner table in the living room of my parent's home. The tree, carved out of wood, was wrapped in white paper and had small handmade candles tied to its branches. Each branch represents a member of the family. It was my favorite Christmas decoration. Now I feel homesick.

December 24

Lightly snowing today. I'm blue because we can't go to a church for *Julotta* in the morning. I have never missed *Julotta* in my life. We have none of the traditional Christmas foods to eat either. At least in Jacksonville we could get *lutfisk* and lingonberries. I didn't even have any milk to make *ostkaka*.

Tonight we read from our Bible and *Psalmbok* and sang some of our favorite Swedish hymns. Carl tried to cheer me up by singing *"Hosianna."* He knows that it's my favorite Christmas song. But the chorus doesn't sound the same with only two people instead of a whole congregation.

Carl carved a 2 foot high *ljus krona* out of scraps of wood. We didn't wrap it with paper this year, but I did tie candles on the three branches. Carl will add more branches as our family grows. Before we went to bed I put the doll under it for Christina to find in the morning. That will be the only present under the *ljus krona* this year.

December 25

I was so happy today to see Benjamin, Adelaide and Laura at the door this morning that I cried. She said "Merry Christmas" and I answered back *"God Jul."* Even though we say it in different languages, we know what the other means. They brought us all presents. When Benjamin gave Carl a pound of coffee, Carl's eyes misted for a second. Adelaide gave me a mold of butter and a pan of *ostkaka*. Carl told her last week about how I had been craving it, so she attempted to make it for me. She even made a sauce out of dried mulberries to put on top. Adelaide had knitted a wool cap for Christina and wrapped it in brown paper. Christina was excited about both the cap and the paper.

They stayed for dinner. I served squirrel stew, potatoes, stewed pumpkin, biscuits, butter and wild plum jam. And we had *ostkaka* for dessert.

This afternoon Mr. Lapsley showed up at the door to say Merry Christmas. I don't know where he got it, but he had a fresh apple for Christina. She was thrilled.

It turned out to be a good Christmas after all. My new neighbors are starting to become "my family."

1869

Families Reunite

January 1

Very cold morning, with a foot of snow on the ground. It was so quiet outside it seemed that the whole world was asleep. The sun glaring off the snow almost blinded me as I stepped out of the dark dugout. The temperature must have been below zero this morning. My nostrils froze as I tried to breathe and I found the water bucket was frozen solid. After I got the outside chores done I tried to do some sewing but my fingers were too cold to do anything without my mittens on. In weather this cold, we stay inside and keep warm. I put so many layers of clothing on Christina that she can hardly move.

January 18

Carl's 30th birthday —The snow quit blowing last night, so Carl could go hunting for fresh meat. We dare not go far from home in this weather unless the sky is clear. With the dugouts low to the ground and covered with snow, it looks like another snowdrift and a person could walk by his own home. Not much wildlife is out in this cold weather, but Carl chanced upon a flock of turkeys and shot one. Besides the meat, we need the feathers to burn for our inside light.

February 20

The sun was out and melted most of the snow from the last blizzard. I was very happy to see Benjamin today. I haven't been off the homestead since Thanksgiving. He stopped by to check on us and give us news. A group of Swedes who formed the First Swedish Agricultural Company of McPherson County have settled about 12 miles to the southwest of us. Because of all the Lind, Lindgren and Lindahl families in the group, they have named the settlement "Lindsborg."

March 5

When Carl went to Salina today for supplies, there was a letter waiting for us from his sister Anna and her husband, Edvin Johnson. They arrived in New York, then traveled to Jacksonville, Illinois. It was a sad letter. Their children—Johan, who was 3, and Denius, just over 1—both died on the ship and were buried at sea. They lost their first child, Clara, in '65 when she was a year old. Anna is due to give birth again next month. Carl is going to write back to them and suggest they come to Kansas. He knows they can't find land in that area and there is still plenty of land here.

The news in town was that Ulysses S. Grant was sworn in as the 18th president of the United States yesterday.

Carl met the new people that live 5 miles northwest of us. Mr. and Mrs. Lars Peterson, sons Peter and Ola, and daughters Betsy and Hannah, have joined the older son Måns, who moved here last October. Bengt Hessler's brothers, Olaf and Sven, also arrived this month.

March 17

Weather is warming up and the days are getting longer. I open the dugout door during the day to let in some fresh air. Yesterday I gave the hides that cover the floor a good shaking to clean some of the dried mud out of the house.

These spring days have seen us outside working on our outbuildings. Carl finally got an outhouse put up for me. With people starting to move into this area, I hate to be out in the open prairie with my skirt up. There are no bushes to hide behind.

Carl has worked the garden, so I started sowing the cool season crops today—cabbage, carrots, peas, lettuce and turnips. I saved seed from last year's garden. I was worried the pack rat would find them.

Adelaide says you must plant the potato eyes at the right time of the moon for the best crop. We plant so much earlier here than in Sweden. We are almost out of potatoes now, and won't have any to harvest until May or June, so we must increase the size of our potato patch.

April 2

I have added to the herb bed I planted by the well last fall. Everyone needs herbs for medicinal use. There is no doctor to help us, so we are on our own when one of us falls sick. The "tonic" plants—the butterfly weed, sweet flagroot and boneset—that I planted last year are starting to send up new shoots from the ground. I planted prairie balm for ointment and Adelaide gave me starts of pennyroyal and horsemint to add to that group. My favorites, the mints for tea, are spreading nicely this spring. I hope to add more herbs for cooking and pickling, both annual and perennial. Dill is the one I need to plant every year for the cucumber pickles.

April 8

It rained today so I knew Carl would be soaked to the bone from his trip to town, but he came home jubilant, waving a letter in the air. It was from Fader saying: "File a homestead claim in my name. We'll be coming to America within the next six months." My parents and my brothers and sisters will be arriving this year! Christina can't figure out why I've been crying if I'm so happy. There is land available to homestead to the west and south of us in this same section. When we left Sweden, I was afraid I'd never see my family again. It made my heart very heavy to think that my parents might never see their grandchildren. It will make life here so much more bearable to have my family here.

April 20

I finally got my setting hen and eggs this week from Adelaide. We didn't have a place for them last year so I had to wait. Carl fashioned a little chicken coop out of lumber scraps and timber from the river. We needed something to shut them in at night so the wild animals don't eat them. Yesterday we heard muffled peeps coming from under the hen. Four eggs have hatched so far. Christina loves to hold the yellow fuzzy chicks in her hands and rub their downy bodies against her face. I have to watch her to see that she doesn't squeeze the poor things to death. At least if she wanders out of my sight, I listen for the cheep of the chicks and I know where to find her.

Mr. Lapsley was over to visit today. He has filed a homestead claim of his own, one mile north and one-half mile west of us along the creek. He is as happy as a lark about it. He plans to build a one-room frame house on his land when he can afford it. Carl said he would help when Larry is ready to start.

May 1

We have increased the acreage of the corn field. Carl had worked the ground last week, then it rained, so we have to wait until the soil dries out to start planting. It is such hard work to break the native grass for the first time. Carl and the ox work so hard. They both need several breaks during the day. I bring coffee or water and bread out at forenoon and afternoon, and a bucket of water for the ox. At noon, they come back to the dugout for a longer rest and the noon meal.

We have increased the field to 10 acres, which means if we get a good crop we could sell the extra to buy supplies. This will also mean more harvesting in the fall, but my brothers can help out this year. We need to plant more of everything this summer since we ran out of some staples last winter. My family also may need food if they don't get here in time to plant their garden. Besides, we will have another mouth to feed.

May 17

Time seems to go slowly waiting for my family to arrive. I have been very tired with this new child in me. Even though it is not officially summer yet, the heat today feels like it. But the garden must be tended just the same. We have been eating lettuce, peas and new onions. The potato plants are blossoming and the corn is up.

I planted the seeds from Christina's Christmas apple at the edge of the garden and they have sprouted. I have been carrying water to the saplings to keep them from withering.

May 31

I'm so happy I could burst! Carl just came home from a trip to Salina and brought a letter from the post office. The return address was Erick Johanson, and it is postmarked Chicago, Illinois. Erick, my other brother, Andrew, and my parents will be coming by train as soon as next week to homestead the land by us. Carl filed on the adjacent 80 acres to the west of us for Fader and to the south of us for Erick. Sara and Emma have found jobs as housemaids in Chicago and will stay there for a while. I think my sisters read our letters about our first year of homesteading, with snakes and all, and have decided

for our brothers to build houses and break the sod before they move
out here.

June 12

It was a scorcher of a Kansas day today. Carl met my parents and
brothers at the train station in Salina. He drove the wagon to haul their
belongings.

I was so happy to see them! I thought I heard someone calling
my name so I went outside and climbed on top of the dugout. In the
distance I saw Andrew standing up in the wagon box, waving his hat
and shouting. When they jumped off the wagon we hugged and cried
and laughed. Christina was a little shy around her *Mormor* and
Morfar, but by evening she was sitting in their laps.

Erick bought a plow in town. We will lend them our ox and we
will use his plow. Fader bought some hand tools, seed wheat, Indian
corn and garden seeds to contribute to the homesteading adventure.
We will share as much as we can with them until they harvest their
first crop and can afford more of their own tools and such.

Fader has decided to make the 80 acres we filed for him a timber
claim since it is along the creek. They will have to plant 1,000 trees
on the acreage to prove it up, but will not have to live on it. Erick will
homestead the north 80 acres of the quarter section south of us, and
my parents will be on the south 80 acres of that same quarter. Since
Andrew is only 18, he cannot file for his own land yet. He says the
day he turns 21—July 14, 1871—he is going to be at the filing office.
We hope there is land close by when he homesteads so we can all still
be neighbors.

June 18

We have been helping Fader and Erick build their sod house. It
is right on the dividing line of their two homesteads, so it counts as
a house on both claims. It is so much more economical to have one
set of household supplies and gather fuel for one fire instead of two.

July 31

Today Moder and I walked over to Adelaide's so they could meet.
Moder does not know any English, so I had to translate the best I
could. Moder looked longingly at Adelaide's rocking chair. She really
hated to leave her furniture behind. The rocking chair in Moder's

house had been used for several generations, but they could not bring it along. She is happy to have the family together again, but she misses her life in Sweden. I understand.

August 4

My time is divided between the garden, Christina, and visits with Moder. Carl spends most of the summer over at the Robinsons'. The payment for this summer's work will be in livestock, a heifer and some young pigs. We need to build a stout pen so the pigs will stay in and the wolves will stay out.

Moder is having a terrible time adjusting to our humid summer heat. I told her to take off some petticoat layers. The less you have on during the summer, the better. We made her a sunbonnet to wear outside when working in her garden.

We have been picking plums, currants, mulberries and grapes this summer as they ripen. I want to dry more than I did last year. Carl bought more crocks so I can make more jams and preserves. I also cut fresh corn off the cob and dried the kernels. Dried corn cooked in cream will hit the spot on a cold day this winter.

August 21

Carl came home with the news today that a Swedish Lutheran Church has been built 10 miles to the northwest of us. A large group of Swedes that had emigrated to Illinois formed the Galesburg Land Company and moved to the bluffs west of the Smoky Hill River. A scout group had been here the year before and bought several sections of land. Most of these settlers are from the Småland and Dalarna provinces, and very poor. I'm told they are very religious people who moved to America because they could not worship God the way they wanted to in Sweden. I hope they can be happy here.

Two months ago they picked the name Salemsborg and immediately started building a dugout church. All work was done by the people who wanted to join the congregation. It is a simple 20-by-40-foot sod building with a rock foundation. The men even carried lumber on their shoulders from Salina for the roof. These people have little money, but they love God and pledged to build a place to worship.

Another group of Swedes from Värmland has settled 7 miles to the west of us. This group is led by a man called Dr. Olof Olsson. He and the members of his Bethany Church are zealous about forming a perfect congregation. No one is allowed to become a member unless he is what they call truly a "Child of God." The church board wasn't sure if Mrs. Olsson even qualified, and she is the pastor's wife. I feel they are carrying their ideas of piety too far. We decided to travel the extra distance and worship with the Salemsborg group instead of the Olsson group.

October 12

Everyone is busy with harvest. I haven't had to help with the wheat sowing or corn harvest as much this year since Erick and Andrew are here. My harvesting in the garden has taken most of my time anyway. The boys dug a root cellar east of the dugout to store our potatoes, root and vine crops. Andrew calls it "the cave," since it is so deep. The pit we dug last year would not hold all of this year's crop, and part of the potatoes froze anyway because the ground freezes so deep during the winter. We do not have enough room in the dugout for food storage and living space too. Soon there will be four people in our house, even if two are children, and we are slowly accumulating more tools and household items that take up space. Occasionally we have travelers stop by that need overnight shelter.

October 27

It is so good to have a milk cow at last! Benjamin said milking the cow is the man's job, but I can do a better job than Carl since boys did not grow up milking cows in Sweden. Helga is a gentle cow and is becoming a good friend. It is so comforting to lay my head against her warm side and listen to the squish of milk as I squeeze her teats.

I made cheese today. It was our custom at home to give the pastor a wheel of cheese for Christmas. This year we have a pastor to give the cheese. It needs to harden between now and Christmas.

November 4

I see that we have accomplished so many things this year when I look around our homestead. Besides our home, we have a shelter for the animals, a crude grain crib and a little chicken coop. Our plowed acres have increased and we have added livestock. I still get lonesome for Sweden, but since my family is here and we are seeing progress on our land, I don't get depressed so often.

November 12

We butchered two of the hogs today, and we had fresh pork and gravy for supper. I was very tired from the work, but the taste of pork made up for it. Part of the meat has been salted to be preserved and we are smoking the hams. Fader and Moder were over to help make the *potatiskorv*. Moder and I chopped potatoes, onions and meat into fine pieces, then Fader stuffed the mixture into the cleaned pig intestines. It is quite a process, but worth it. He used an old buffalo horn with the end cut out to hold the intestines open, then stuffed the mixture with his other hand until the intestines was full. You must watch so you don't overstuff the intestine and burst it. Fader has had lots of years of practice. We boiled the *potatiskorv*, then fried it in lard until the skin was golden brown and crisp. We always have to have a taste right out of the frying pan, but this is one of the special meats we save for our Christmas Eve *smörgåsbord*.

November 28

Today is the first church service at the Salemsborg Church. We started out early this morning in the wagon. Pastor A.W. Dahlsten is serving our congregation, and we enjoyed his sermon. The wine and bread sacraments were the first we had received since we left Illinois a year and a half ago. I'm afraid the distance and the weather will keep us from attending church regularly, but it does my heart and soul good to know we have a place to go.

The pastor had hoped to start the church services last month, but we had an unusual amount of rain and the sod walls of the church caved in on October 2nd. The men had to build the church again before it was ever used. This time they hauled down stone from the bluffs for the walls. The floor is still earth, and it was a muddy mess today because of last week's rains.

December 25

We went to *Julotta* this morning. Church starts at 5 a.m. on this special day, so we did our chores in the middle of the night and left at 3 a.m. Moder fussed, saying I shouldn't be out in my condition since my baby could come any day, but I couldn't miss being at church this morning! It was a clear cold night with a full moon. Carl fitted the wagon box on sleds so we could slide across the snow. The moonlight glowing on the snow added to the magic of the holiday. I heated rocks in the fire to put beneath our feet in the wagon for warmth. Christina was so bundled up, I had to remember she was tucked away under the buffalo robes.

Candles beamed from homestead windows that we passed, just like in Sweden, where we would set out the candles at 4 a.m. to light the way for the people in our parish walking to *Julotta*. The candle glow in the dark was comforting.

Salemsborg Church was full of people that were spending their first Christmas away from their homeland. Many hearts and minds were back in their homes in Sweden. I was not the only person who had tears in her eyes as we sung our traditional hymns.

This year we celebrated Christmas with all the trimmings and traditions of our family. I'll admit we used a primitive substitute for most of our Christmas dishes, but Moder makes the best *ostkaka* and *frukt soppa* no matter where she lives. Adelaide gave us some white sugar to make some *kringler*, the pastry Carl likes. Since we butchered a hog this fall, we had *potatiskorv* and a smoked ham also. I pickled catfish we caught in the river this fall and mixed it with potatoes and beets for Fader's favorite dish of *sillsallad*. It doesn't quite taste the same since it is supposed to be made with herring, but he was happy. This Christmas is so different from last year. What a difference family can make.

1870

Building the House

January 1

There is a skiff of snow on the ground, but the weather hasn't turned bad yet. The year may show many changes as our family and homestead grow. We hope to plow more acres and start on our house, and, of course, I hope to have a healthy new baby soon.

The first service in Dr. Olsson's new stone church was today. It is near the *bolagshuset*. People at the Salemsborg church were talking about Dr. Olsson's strict beliefs. I believe it will cause strife among the people in the future.

January 4

Our son Anders Wilhelm was born in the dugout today. He is named after Carl's little brother, Johan Wilhelm. Willie has dark hair like mine and strong lungs. His cries fill our small dugout. Carl wanted to go out in the middle of the night last night to get Moder, but I told him the trip could wait until daylight because it could be hours before the birth. It is not far to her house if he takes the horse, but the wind has been blowing the snow and I did not need them to get lost. Moder got here at dawn, in time to help with the delivery and look after Christina when she woke up. Carl was so happy to get a son. At the moment I'm just thankful that the baby is healthy and I survived the delivery.

January 23

Bundled up the children for the ride to Salemsborg Church. Willie was baptized today by Pastor Dahlsten. Since it was so cold in the church I unwrapped the baby just long enough for the short ceremony, then quickly bundled him up again. My family was present as sponsors, meaning they promise to raise our child if something would happen to Carl and I.

My routine and spare time has changed with a new baby to take care of besides the milking and other chores. Christina watches him if I need to be outside for something. There is not much she can do except run and get me if Willie crys. I think she is feeling a little threatened by Willie. After he is down for a nap, she wants to crawl into my lap for a moment of undivided attention. I spend a lot of time washing diapers. I only have a few that I made from old flour sacks, so I must boil water and wash every day.

February 25

My sisters got here yesterday from Chicago. Fader and Moder met them at the depot in Salina. I couln't believe how much Sara and Emma have changed, but it has been three years since I saw them. They had so many stories about the city of Chicago and the families they worked for. They both could speak better English than me, even though I have been practicing with Adelaide. Sara and Emma last saw Christina when she was 3 months old. She was shy around them at first, but Christina warmed up to her aunts quickly after Emma gave her a lump of sugar. It is so good to see them again.

March 3

Carl was very solemn when he came back from Salina today. He didn't say anything, just handed me a letter he received from his parents and walked off toward the creek. Enclosed was a death card trimmed in black bearing the news that Carl's brother Anders Magnus had died. He was just 24.

Christina has a cold this week. I made a mustard plaster to smear on her chest, and I covered it with a piece of wool flannel. The mustard can blister a child's tender skin but it usually does the trick to draw the cold out of the body. I hope the baby does not get Christina's cold. When one of the children get sick I worry so. I wish there was a doctor in our area.

March 20

I spent the day cutting up potatoes to plant tomorrow. It was so nice today, just a soft warm breeze and a clear blue sky. I wish spring weather could last forever. Christina found a nest of baby bunnies today. They were so tiny they didn't have their eyes open yet. She wanted to pick them up, but I told her the momma bunny would not take care of them if she touched them.

March 21

Planted the potato eyes and some more vegetables today. A shower of rain passed over us this evening. That was perfect timing. I hope we get a good crop this year.

Carl's family will be joining us soon. *Svärfar* and *Svärmor* will bring Emma, Emanuel, Johan and Elenora. They range in age from 18 to 11. They will be crossing the ocean on the Cunard Line steamer to New York, then taking the train to Kansas.

I never thought we'd see Sven Magnus and Katarina Andersson come to America. Svärfar owned part of the original land that King Carl the Twelfth of Sweden gave Halfward Bryngelsson (Svärfar's ancestor) back in 1716. They live in a mansion by our standards. Tenants farmed Svärfar's land for him. I imagine he plans to buy a vast track of land in Kansas and build a large home.

All of their older children are emigrating to America, so maybe that is the reason they decided to leave Sweden. The four oldest daughters are married and have children. Lena and Olof Danielsson, Anna and Edvin, and Clara and Otto Peterson are going to settle in this area. Sara Lisa and Johannes Brentson have already settled in Iowa.

April 6

I had five stray longhorns near the dugout today when I came back from the field. I was hoping they would wander on by themselves, but when one steer climbed on top of the dugout I lost my fear of those long horns and sprang into action. My children were inside the dugout and I could imagine what could happen if the roof caved in from the weight of the cattle. I screamed at the top of my lungs, snapped my apron in the air and ran straight toward them. Of course when they bolted off, they scattered into the corn field, crashing five paths of corn stalks to the ground.

Charles and Emma Lamkin have filed on the land west of us along the river. Erick and Fader have neighbors to the west of them now too—the Thomas Husted and the Magnus Fager families have filed homestead claims there.

Carl heard that Bothilda Hessler has arrived to live on the homestead claim her brothers had filed for her. I did not know until today that she will be marrying Måns Peterson.

April 19

The field work continues. Carl is breaking more sod for corn, rye and wheat. With more animals, we need more feed. Carl will be spending most of next week at the Robinsons' to help plant their corn. I hope we can get our corn planted first. I have been outside to help as much as I can. Moder comes to watch the baby and Christina, or I set the cradle outside so I can keep an eye on Willie.

May 4

Carl's parents and family have arrived. They stayed in Illinois for a short while before getting back on the train for Kansas. Carl met them at the depot in Salina. While they were in town, Svärfar applied for his citizenship papers and filed a homestead claim on the section northeast of us. Svärmor is not impressed with Kansas, the weather or our home. She about fainted when she saw the dugout.

Svärfar and Svärmor will be living with us while Carl and his brothers build a dugout for them. All the men and boys can sleep outside, but that will be six more people to feed and find bedding for. It seems Svärfar did not realize the cost of paying for the family to travel to America, and now he is short of funds to build a real house. Anna and Edvin are not here yet. They are coming by covered wagon instead of spending the money on train tickets. It is good to see Carl's family again.

May 20

Carl's family has moved into its own dugout. Our home seems so large now. It was good to have them here to visit, but I'm glad to have my place back to the four of us.

The weather is slowly warming up, and the garden and corn have sprouted. If I can keep the jackrabbits out of the garden, I will have a better stand. Last night they ate down a whole row of peas. I believe I'm ready for some rabbit stew.

June 4

We finally have enough stone to start building our house. We have been collecting sandstone rocks whenever we come across them in the field or the creek. It has been hard to find enough rock nearby.

Yesterday Carl picked up the last wagonload of local rock. There is a rise of hills two miles south that has an outcropping of stone. The rains last week loosened the sod enough that it was easy to dig out the rocks with a spade and pick.

The cellar is dug. It will be used as storage for our preserved food, and as a root cellar for our vegetables and fruits from the garden. We also need a place for shelter from tornadoes, the cyclone winds that Kansas is known for. We'll have one entrance to the cellar from outside on the north, one from the porch on the south and one inside the house. After the stone walls are in place in the cellar, and the floor is laid for the house, I want to move into the cellar. We'd have more room than in the dugout and the cellar floor seems drier than the dugout floor. We have had water seeping up from the floor of the dugout this spring. It is always muddy and doesn't want to dry out. It will be so nice to get out of the damp ground and live on a wooden floor when the house is done.

Our house will measure 16 feet square. Imagine all the space we'll have. It will consist of one big room with a loft above it. We hope to add on more rooms as we have the time and money.

Carl bought glass for three windows, a door, shingles and more lumber when he was in Salina last week. One window will go in the middle of the west wall, one in the middle of the south wall, and a little window in the west end of the loft. The front door will go in the southeast corner of the house.

Carl also bought a big cooking stove with the money he received from selling some of last year's wheat. It will go on the west wall, just to the right of the window so I can gaze out at our farm while I'm cooking.

We'll have a ladder on the east wall to get up into the loft, which we'll use as storage and for an extra bedroom. I'd like to add a porch to the south eventually. Then I can sit and watch the children play while I'm sewing, snapping beans or whatever needs to be done.

June 12

Rock by rock we are slowly building the walls. We are mixing a plaster of sand, clay and lime to cement the rock together. Benjamin and Mr. Lapsley are helping today. Adelaide came over to watch the progress and help me fix the meals for the extra hands.

As I stood inside my partially built house tonight, I tried to imagine what it will look like when it is done. I want to put up red gingham curtains that I can tie back during the day, and braid some rag rugs for the floor. The old hides have worked well in the dugout, but I want our new home to look like a real house, like the one we had in Sweden.

June 16

We had a hailstorm today. It made me sick to my stomach to watch our crops get beaten down. The wheat field is half as tall as it was yesterday. It was almost ripe, so we can still harvest it, but it will be a stooping, back-breaking job since the stems are bent or broken off. We will have to rake up the crop instead of binding it in bundles. The young corn leaves were shredded, so the yield will be decreased. The plants are young, so the crop was not destroyed. The potato vines were broken, but the potatoes were already developing underground so they should be fine. The vine plants had started to sprout, and I might have to replant again. I got them in late this year. I'm worried about the tomato plants the most. The stems are so pitted from the hail that they might not survive, and it is almost too late to replant them.

We lost two chickens that were caught in the storm and got pelted to death by the hailstones. Carl was over at the Robinsons' when the storm hit. Their crops were damaged too. We didn't need this, God. We were counting on that food and income.

July 14

A census taker stopped our work today. He wanted information about our family for the 1870 census. The census taker listed our names in Saline County, Walnut Grove Township, as Swenson, Charles—age 30, Anna—26, Christine—3 and William—1/2 year.

He put Carl's name in the American version—Charles Swenson. We tried to correct his mistakes when he wrote them down, but we couldn't get him to understand our Swedish. I told him my name was Maja Kajsa, not Anna, and our daughter's name is Anna Christina. And he had Carl's age wrong too. Oh well, it won't matter a 100 years from now what they put our names down as in 1870.

August 3

Svärmor is having a fit. The snakes and fleas are about to drive the woman insane. I remember our first year, and how we survived, but she doesn't seem to want to even try. I try to help her out, but her attitude tries my patience at times. If she keeps spending all of Svärfar's money on food, instead of raising it herself, they are going to be in that dugout a long time.

August 22

We moved out of the cellar and into our house today! We have so much room compared to the dugout. And clean floors, not mud. Bright sunshine pours through the clean glass windows. The stove gleams, ready to use in its corner space. Next Carl will have to build some furniture to fill up our house. I want a big table, with a bench on either side, to go in the southwest part of the room. I need a bin near the stove for the chips and kindling. A cupboard on the north wall would be handy for my cooking utensils and food supplies. Our bed will be in the northeast end, with a trundle bed to pull out for the children. And we need a wardrobe or dresser for our clothes. That can go on the east wall beside the loft ladder. I thank the Lord we finally have a real house after two years.

September 5

Rainy day. Nice to spend time inside for a change. We have been so busy this summer, with the crops and garden, and building our house. Two years ago I was out on the prairie all by myself. Now my family or Carl's drop by for coffee or a visit almost every day.

It has been fun to preserve food with my new stove and to have a big cellar to store it in. Granted the house gets hot, compared to the cool dugout, but I am so happy to have a wood floor to stand on and a stove and oven to cook with. It is worth the discomfort.

Our crop yields were down because of the June hailstorm, but the garden recovered fairly well. I'm glad the hail didn't come later in the season.

November 2

First snow today. It came down slow and silent, gigantic flakes drifting from the sky at their own pace. So different than the snows we get during a blizzard. I am just about done with the rag rug I started before corn snapping. Seems like it took quite a while to tear the old clothing into the strips for the braid, but now as I sew the braid around in an oval it is going faster. This rug will go in front of our bed.

My next project will be a new cloak for me and altering some of Christina's clothes for Willie. I hate to spend our money on material, but my cloak is threadbare and I need a warm coat when I am out in the winter. Moder offered to watch the children the next time Carl goes to town, so I can go along and pick out the material. I have not been to Salina in almost a year.

Carl ordered *lutfisk* from the general store for our Christmas dinner, so he needs to pick that up along with supplies we will need for the winter. It is such a long trip that he goes only when absolutely necessary. We will pick up supplies for our families also.

December 24

Our first Christmas Eve in our new house. It looks so festive with cedar boughs hanging above the windows. The air is scented with a freshness that reminds me of Sweden. The *ljus krona* is sporting a fourth branch this year for Willie.

Both sides of the family came here tonight for the *smörgåsbord,* since we have the biggest house of the family. Everyone brought food to share and we had a wonderful time. Each Christmas gets better in America.

December 25

When we left for Salemsborg Church this morning for *Julotta,* Carl's family headed in the opposite direction for Bethany Church. I'm glad we celebrated Christmas together last night.

1871

Naturalization Papers

January 27

It has been a quiet winter, without any harsh snowstorms. Carl has been working on the barn on the warmer days. He is adding a lean-to on the south side. We need a place to milk the cow, and we must have stalls for the horses and oxen. On bad weather days, there are endless little tasks to be done: fix the harness, build shelves in the house, twist hay for fuel. The jobs never cease for either of us. Besides taking care of the children, the cooking, baking and washing, I spend my winter mending or making over our old clothes for the children and knitting our year's supply of stockings and mittens.

February 8

Svärfar came over with news today. Anna and Edvin have a new baby, called Emma Mathilda. I hope the little girl stays well. I plan to go over tomorrow to help with the cooking.

We have a new four-legged addition to our family. A wagon came through here this week and stopped for water for the oxen. They had a young dog that was having trouble keeping up with them. The pads on his paws were cracked and bloody from walking in the ice and snow. They feared the dog would not make it to their destination, so they asked us to give it a home. We have needed a dog to protect the homestead so we were happy to take it. There are few dogs in this part of the county, except the Indians' dogs. This pup has some growing to do, but seems to be smart. He whined when the wagon left him behind, but I'm sure Christina will make him feel at home here. She has named him Spot. He has a golden brown shaggy coat, except for the one white spot on his forehead and a tuft of white on his chest.

February 28

Måns Peterson and Bothilda Hessler were married by the Rev. Bartels in Salina today. Bothilda got her naturalization papers last Thursday, the 23rd. She had to get her papers, since she filed for homestead land. In a single week she became both a wife and an American citizen. They are a nice couple, but they live 5 miles away, so the only time we see them is at church.

Since we have had some days of thawing sun, Carl has been helping Erick build his house. It is a one-room stone house, with a half room upstairs. Since he is a bachelor, he doesn't need a very big house.

The men start out with several layers of clothing in the morning, but by noon they have warmed up and have taken off their coats. When I was at Moder's today to help with the meal, I noticed the grass was starting to green up on the south side of their sod house. It is so good to see signs of spring and feel the sun penetrating my skin. I would not say that in the middle of summer, but it feels so good at the end of winter.

March 14

One of our goals this year is to start enclosing our fields by planting hedge trees around the perimeters. With all the cattle drives in the area, we need to protect our crops. We don't have money for a board plank fence to go around 80 acres. It would not stop a stampeding herd anyway. There are some Osage Orange trees down at the river. They are native to the area and will make good protection. These hedge trees grow thick, with thorns on their branches. A dense stand can hold out any longhorn. Last fall, we fought the squirrels and gathered as many hedge apples as we could to plant this spring.

A traveling salesman came through at about the same time, and he said he would be carrying saplings for sale next time he is in this area. We might trade him some food or eggs for hedge or fruit trees. We like the creek plums, but I would love to have some peach and pear trees. Three apple trees sprouted from the seeds I planted two years ago from Christina's Christmas apple. I wrapped the little twigs with newspaper last fall, but the rabbits gnawed through and girdled two of the trees. I hope the other sapling makes it.

March 30

It misted early this morning, but quit by the time Carl and Andrew left to get our spring supplies in town. We rarely get mail now that the family lives in Kansas, but Carl's naturalization papers were waiting in the mail. He proudly waved the paper in front of me when he walked in the door tonight. It is official as of March 20, 1871. Carl's name on his paper reads Charles John Swenson. Legally he is no longer Carl Johan Svensson. He had to apply for the naturalization papers to file for homestead land. I did not apply for papers, because I don't want to lose my ties with Sweden.

April 10

At the annual church meeting today, it was decided to increase the pastor's salary. To do so, each family must donate three bushels of wheat in addition to the church dues. We pray for a better crop and harvest than we received from the Lord last year.

May 12

The garden is up and so is Willie. He is starting to toddle around the house. If Christina and Willie are outside, Spot is right beside Willie, almost like he is ready to catch the baby the next time he tumbles over.

Spot has turned into a handsome, faithful dog. His only downfall has been "helping" me plant the potato eyes this year. For every 10 potato eyes I planted, he tried to dig up two. I would yell and threaten and Spot would just run in a wide circle, stop, spin around and run again. The children joined in the act and it took forever to finish planting.

We have dug up currant bushes from the creek and planted them on the north side of the house. Besides having currants handy for picking, I wanted some plantings around the house. I love to pause to sniff the sweet scent of the flowers.

May 23

My cousin Peter Olson has homesteaded 80 acres, a mile south and a mile east of us. We grew up together in Sweden. Peter has dug a dugout and is now clearing and planting his land.

Actually, Peter came to America in '68, a year after us, but is just getting to Kansas. When he decided to leave Sweden, he sold his cattle in Norway to get a better price. Peter said he was scared walking back home with all that money in his pocket. He left behind his parents and sisters for now, but he hopes to send for them.

Peter stopped in Missouri to help build the railroads. He quit that job though, because they wanted him to work Sundays, which we know is the Lord's day of rest.

Peter traveled to Kansas by train, along the Missouri-Kansas-Texas line. In a notebook he recorded the depots along the way—Emporia, White City, Skittle. Since we came through Chicago, we did not go through those towns.

July 3

Wheat harvest has progressed without any problems this year. The bundles are stacked and ready to thresh. We have had some huge thunderheads build up in the west, but thankfully they have dissipated instead of producing a storm.

A school has been built by the Petersons and Hesslers, but 5 miles is too far for Christina to walk to get there. She would be old enough to start next year if the school were closer. I am teaching her to read and count.

July 14

Andrew celebrated his 21st birthday by becoming an official landowner. Andrew talked Sara into signing the homestead papers for him this spring, so he could get in the spring crop on the land. She signed it over to him on his birthday. His land is to the southeast of Fader on the next section. He also filed for a timber claim next to his 80 acres. Andrew wants to build a log house in the future.

August 8

It was sweltering today. The children and I walked over to the Robinsons' for a visit. Coming back, Christina was hot and tired and Willie was fussing. I was at the end of my patience. Finally, Christina lay down on the ground and refused to go another step. I pleaded, threatened and bribed, but she just laid there crying. I couldn't carry them both the last half mile. Finally I told Christina to stay put and not move.

I ran home as fast as I could carry Willie and put him in his bed. Then I ran back to where I left Christina, praying she had not gotten up and wandered off in the tall grass. I was already hot and sweaty, but by the time I ran a mile I was about ready to pass out. Christina had gotten scared and was starting to wander toward home when I got back to her. I picked her up and carried her home. I was even more worried with Willie by himself.

The worst things go through your mind when you think about what could happen to your children. What if Christina gets lost in the tall grass, gets bit by a rattlesnake, charged by a buffalo, dragged off by a wolf? What if an Indian takes Willie out of his crib and sets the house on fire? I have heard of such things happening to the settler children. I will never let either child out of my sight again.

September 20

The men folk have started working on Fader and Moder's house. It will be a wood-frame house with three rooms downstairs and a room upstairs. They plan to get the outside work down this fall and finish the inside this winter in their spare time. Moder is anxious to get out of their sod house. She had hoped to be in the new house before now, but fieldwork has first priority.

December 25

Christmas has arrived and another year is about to end. The church was bulging with people this morning for *Julotta*, because the weather was decent. Our congregation has grown steadily this year as more Swedish emigrants homestead in the county. It is so fun to meet the newcomers and ask what district in Sweden they are from. If someone was from our area, I asked questions like "What is going on in Sweden now? Who married who? Any new babies or deaths in the families we might know?" There is a bond that ties us all together because we are from the same country, even if we didn't know each other before. One woman was so unhappy, but I told her things will get better with time. As I was consoling her, I realized that I am beginning to think of America as my home.

We have had a lot to be thankful for this year. I pray that God will watch over us into the new year and keep us well.

1872

Visit from the Indians

February 21

I am not writing in my journal as often as I did the first years here on the homestead. Then I needed a way to release my loneliness and fears. Now I seem to get the urge to write when there is an event in the family, or a bit of important news. My life has changed dramatically over the past five years and I can see that when I read through my old journals.

March 24

Carl's 16-year-old brother Johan was confirmed today by Dr. Olsson at Bethany Church. We went along for the confirmation service. It was so nice to visit with several neighbors that we don't see very often, since we don't go to this church. Dr. Olsson has organized a youth choir that sang a beautiful anthem today. He has a knack for organizing the young people in his congregation.

April 15

Carl stopped at Måns Peterson's on the way home from Salina today. Bothilda had a baby boy on April 3rd. They named him Carl August.

We also heard that an iron bridge is going to be built over the river to the south to the of us near the grist mill. The Lamer brothers have pushed this project and have taken up subscriptions from the people in the area. We use the ford across the river straight west of us when the river is low. It will be nice to have a bridge when the water is too high to cross.

May 6

Sara has married Claus Sjogren. They will be farming over by Salemsborg Church, so we won't see them as often as before they were married. We can visit after church service on Sundays. I like Claus. He always has a twinkle in his eye and a smile on his lips.

July 25

Summer has disappeared into the busy season. When I am hoeing in the garden, Christina helps by pulling weeds or keeping track of Willie, although that is still Spot's job. When I need a rest, we work on Christina's lettering. She draws the alphabet in the soil with a weed stem. She gets so far, then Spot and Willie charge through, their feet erasing her efforts. I am expecting another child in the winter. My energy level has been low, but I have to get my work done anyway.

October 30

Today we made our years' supply of soap. I had been saving the fire ashes for the lye, and lard from my cooking all year. I hate this job and hate to have the children in the area when we make soap. Lye burns the skin, and the throat if it is inhaled. After the mixture boiled to the right consistency, we poured it into pans to cool and harden. Tomorrow I will cut the soap into squares and wrap the squares in straw to store them in the cellar.

November 20

We are used to seeing our Indian neighbors fairly often. After all, they have lived along the river for generations. I know that a tribe camped down by the river in earlier times, because we have found arrowheads in the field after the spring rains.

It was dusk last night when two husky young Indians knocked on our door. They were wrapped in their buffalo robes. We had several inches of snow on the ground, and it was going to be a very cold night. Luckily, Carl was in the house so I didn't have to try to understand their talk and motions. They wanted a place to spend the night. Carl said that they would be welcome if they gave him their guns for the night. Carl fed and tied the horses in our barn, and the Indians made their beds on the kitchen floor by the stove.

Although we didn't sleep well, I believe the two young men did. I made extra breakfast to include them in our meal. They ate in silence, devouring a big plate of eggs, ham and bread. The children stared wide-eyed at our guests during the whole meal. The Indians rose from the table as soon as they were done eating, even though the rest of us were not finished. Carl led them out to the barn for their horses and guns. I gave them a parcel of flour, meat and raw potatoes so they could prepare a meal later in the day. Silently the Indians mounted their horses and rode to the west.

When Carl was down by the creek, he found the potatoes I had given the Indians. Apparently, potatoes aren't their favorite food.

The buffalo, the Indians' main food supply, have almost been wiped out of this area. I know the Indians are having a hard time feeding and clothing their own families without the herds.

We need to be friendly to these people. They lived on this land first. Still, settlers along the Kentucky Creek have been killed during Indian raids, so we should never turn our backs to them.

December 12

The snow has quit and has formed a crust so it won't be blowing into drifts. It is unusual to see snow so level here. The prairie winds seem to blow summer and winter. Icicles are forming on the west side of the house from the sun melting the snow on the roof. When I went to the outhouse this afternoon, the icicles sparkled so brightly it made me squint. I broke off a couple for the children to suck on as a treat.

Adelaide and Laura visited today and brought us some apples as an early Christmas present. Benjamin had bought several bushels this fall in Salina. She made the apples into apple butter, or dried rings, but had kept the best for eating this winter.

1873

Willie's Shoes

January 2

It was so cold today, I think the mercury was frozen in the bottom of the thermometer. Add the chill of the wind and you have a day no man or beast should be out. It is so bad, there is a quarter-inch of ice on the *inside* of the windows. Carl made sure all of the animals were fed and locked up in the barn, then spent the rest of the day with us in the house. Even with the stove going full blast, it is barely keeping the house warm enough for the children.

January 27

Our new daughter, Alma Eleanor, was born this cold morning. Moder was with me, but it was an easy birth. Alma has blonde hair and the prettiest eyes. It is such a joy to hold my newborn that I forgot the pain I went through to bring her into this world. Christina was happy to have new sister. Moder will keep the children for a few days so I can spend time with my new little one.

January 30

Anna and Edvin have a new baby. Axel is the sixth child she has given birth to. We were wondering which baby would be born first, theirs or ours.

February 9

We traveled to Salemsborg today to have Alma baptized. I wish the church was not so far away. It is so cold to have the baby out, but she had to be baptized.

February 14

Sara gave birth to Franz Oskar Sjogren today. This is the third new baby in our family in a month's time.

We finally got a break in the weather. It was such a miserable winter, I spent most of the last two months indoors. Carl milked the cows for me, since I am busy with the baby and he does not have field work to do this time of year. He even churned butter last week when I wasn't feeling well. We have had a round of colds this winter. I have brewed many cups of Moder's cold remedy. I boil together catnip, horehound and onions, and attempt to sweeten it with honey. It is bitter, but it helps soothe the throat and clear the nose. Christina has had an earache for two days. To help relieve the pressure in her ear, I baked a potato and had her lay her ear on it. The steam from the hot potato helped ease the pain.

March 3

The geese are flying north today, so spring is around the corner. We ran outside to scan the sky when we heard the honks of the first flock overhead. The V-shaped formation of the geese was flying back to their nesting grounds, wherever that might be.

A little village has sprung up around the grist mill at the old Indian river crossing a few miles southwest of us. Huge herds of longhorn cattle are driven up from Texas to Salina, where they are shipped by railroad to the Eastern states. The rangers stop the cattle in this bend by the mill to rest and be watered before they move on to Salina. The mooing of thousands of cattle drifts through the early evening if the wind is in the right direction. So does the smell.

March 23

Seventeen people from our southeast church district met at Bengt Hessler's to talk about starting a church separate from the Salemsborg Church. Bengt will donate two acres of his land for the church and cemetery site. It will be a good location for members on both sides of the river. The plan is to save enough money to build a church two years from now. We will support the new church.

April 21

We have new neighbors two miles south of us: Eric Carlson and his sons Olof, Swan and Charlie, and the hired girl, Ellen.

Eric told me his first wife died after their daughter, Hannah, was born. He remarried and had five more children, but then his second wife also died. The two younger daughters stayed in Sweden.

The family left Kyrkhult, Sweden, in '71, and stayed in Chicago for a while. Hannah found work as a maid for an Episcopalian minister and his family, so she stayed there.

They told us about the great fire in Chicago that happened two years ago. I just shuddered when Eric told how the whole city was burning around them. They were lucky to escape.

May 24

Dr. Olsson is publishing a Christian monthly periodical called *Nytt och Gammalt.* The communities need a newspaper and he is a good writer. Svärfar has shared his copies with us.

Carl's parents hope to build a house soon, but I don't know if it will materialize this year. Svärfar is not a farmer and has not had good luck with his crops. Carl tries to help out, but we have our hands full with all the work that needs to be done here.

June 15

Carl bought me a new 10-gallon butter churn for my birthday. Now I can churn a bigger batch of butter all at once. Our three cows are producing enough for us to have fresh milk to drink and cream for butter. I let the milk sit in crocks in the cave for a few days to let the cream rise to the top. Then I can skim it off and churn the butter. I want to make extra butter and sell it at the village by the grist mill. The skim milk is fed to the pigs and Spot.

July 17

I was hoeing in the garden today when Spot started to bark. We get travelers now and then as they pass through. They need a place to stay for the night or just water for themselves or the animals. The man who stopped today was from Lindsborg. He said he heard that the last old buffalo had been shot in our Smoky Valley region. The animals were so plentiful a decade ago and now they are gone.

September 4

I am going to get enough apples off of Christina's Christmas apple tree this year for one pie. This is the first year that the tree has produced. Christina has been checking the coloring of the apples every day to see if they are ready to pick.

The hedge trees around our fields are showing good growth this year. We had to replant a few gaps, but overall the farm is taking shape.

We have started building the granary. We have 40 acres in crops, so we need permanent storage for the grain. In the past, we have used part of the barn, but as we add more livestock the space is needed for the animals. During the summer, they are in the meadow by the creek, but during the winter we like to have the horses, milk cows and sows inside.

November 11

Two prairie schooners pulled into our yard yesterday. They were heading south and needed a place to stay for the night. One wagon had a family of 10 and the other had a young couple with a newborn baby. It is so sad to see travelers in this cold November weather. The little children weren't dressed warm enough and one little boy, about Willie's age, was barefoot. I felt so sorry for them, but we don't have much to spare in the way of clothing.

The young mother and baby spent the night in our kitchen where it is warm. The rest of the group camped in the out buildings.

Carl had just finished a new pair of brass-capped shoes for Willie this week and Willie just had to show them off to the visiting children. Carl told Willie to give the shoes to the barefoot boy this morning before the family left. Our son needed a new pair of shoes, but not as badly as that little boy.

The little stranger was so excited when Willie finally held out the shoes. The boy took a couple of rags that I had just cleaned the stove with and wrapped them around his feet before he put on the shoes. I didn't realize until then that the child probably didn't have any socks either.

December 7

Christina's 7th birthday —She has been a big help to me this year with Alma. When I asked Christina what she wanted for her birthday, she replied, "A batch of *smörbakelser* all for myself." I use a common butter cookie dough, roll it out thin, cut it in circles, and form a little cup with an edge around it. I whip sugar and egg whites to form a stiff peak and fold in chopped black walnuts. A dallop of the egg mixture is spooned into each cup and they are sprinkled with a little sugar on top. I have been saving sugar for the Christmas baking, so I used some for her cookies. We also gave her a red satin ribbon for her hair.

It was a treat for all of us today to have Emma's and Sara's here for dinner. Sara told us about the Mission Friends' Church that they helped organize in September. They plan to build a church a mile north of the Salemsborg Church. We will miss them at our church, but we can see them after we both get out of our services.

Smörbakelser

2 cups butter
1 cup sugar
1 whole egg and 1 yolk
egg whites
3-4 cups flour
chopped nuts

Cream butter until soft. Add sugar and blend well. Add whole egg and yolk together. Add enough flour to handle. Cut dough into circles and cup edges. Make filling of beaten egg whites, sugar and nuts and fill cookies. Sprinkle with sugar. Bake until light brown.

Pepparkakor

3/4 cup lard
1 cup sugar
1/4 cup molasses
1 egg
2 teaspoon soda
2 cups flour
1/2 teaspoon cloves
1/2 teaspoon ginger
1 teaspoon cinnamon
1/2 teaspoon salt

Melt lard in pan. Add rest of ingredients. Make into balls and roll in sugar. Bake until done.

1874

Grasshoppers

January 4

Willie's 4th birthday—He asked for *pepparkakor* for his treat. He remembered Christina got cookies on her birthday. Willie helped me mix the molasses cookie dough. I did let him put a pinch of sugar on top of the cookies before we baked them, but he got carried away and used too much before I could stop him. I didn't scold him, since he was excited about his birthday, but we won't be to town for several weeks for supplies and will have to use our sugar sparingly.

February 17

The weather is mild this winter, so we have gotten an early start on the room we are adding to the north side of the house. Right now, all we can afford to do is build a large lean-to with a flat roof. We must get by as inexpensively as possible. We will move the cooking stove into the new room and make it the kitchen. The little stove we used in the dugout will heat the original room. I would like Carl to build a wall of shelves or cupboards on the south wall in the kitchen, but right now I am happy just to be getting another room.

March 26

It's been an exciting few days around the neighborhood. Hannah Carlson left today after a short visit with her family. She really likes her job and the lifestyle in Chicago, but her father summoned her to Kansas.

Eric has picked a husband for her—my cousin, Peter. She's never even met Peter, and he lives in a dugout out in the middle of nowhere.

Why should she give up her comfortable life in Chicago for a hole in the ground?

April 1

Svärfar and Svärmor have left Bethany Church. Several members of the congregation left recently because they do not agree with Dr. Olsson and the church council's strict rules and views. Carl's family will start going to the Salemsborg Church with us.

The wheat does not look very good this spring. We had a mild winter and didn't have much snow cover on the crop. There are two bare patches in the field where the wind blew the wheat out. We need a good soaking rain.

May 26

We read in the paper today that President Grant's daughter, Nellie, was married to a wealthy Englishman in a grand White House ceremony on the 21st. I can't imagine living a wealthy life and having people do the work for me. I shouldn't daydream about it, because it will never happen to us.

I have to think of more practical things. I'm afraid the dry spring means a hot summer ahead. The part of the garden that I am watering looks good, but I cannot carry water to the whole acre. The child that I'm carrying makes my back ache. I hope this pregnancy is not worse than the others.

July 19

Olaf Hessler and Elsa Peterson were married by Pastor Dahlsten at Salemsborg today. Elsa and her 6-year-old daughter came across from Jämshög earlier this year. I haven't gotten to know her yet, but I wonder if she is any relation to the Lars Peterson family?

I am carrying water to the fruit trees. The leaves look withered and gray. Most of the tree blossoms were damaged in a late freeze, so we will not get much fruit this year. Maybe one peach pie and a half-bushel of apples is all I can hope for now.

July 27

It is all gone! I'm surprised I have a pencil and paper to write on after the horrors of today. It started innocently enough. Christina and I picked beans this morning and had brought them into the kitchen while Carl and Willie stacked fresh hay south of the barn. All of a sudden, a huge dark cloud blotted out the sun.

Before Carl and Willie got to the house, they were being pelted, but it wasn't rain. It was millions of grasshoppers falling from the sky. In minutes, grasshoppers were everywhere! We shut the windows and doors immediately, but hundreds were already inside the house. Outside they were crawling on everything. Our crops and garden were being devoured in front of our eyes!

Carl and I shouted to the children to stay inside as we made a dash for the garden to pick as many vegetables as we could. The insects were all over us, blinding us, biting and crawling inside of our clothing. The sound of their chewing was deafening and I felt in a panic. I couldn't walk without crushing bunches with every step.

When the hoard finally moved on hours later, there was neither bark nor a leaf left on our trees. The only things left on my fruit trees were three peach stones. The garden had been devoured, even the onions beneath the ground! Whole watermelons disappeared. Our fields of corn were reduced to nothing but a few stumps. Anything that had any moisture in it was consumed. Even part of the fresh-cut haystack was gone, as was the handle of the pitchfork that Carl had dropped by the stack.

My wash was on the line, but you could not tell what it was by the fragments left behind. Inside, the grasshoppers were eating the curtains, the beans we brought in and the fresh loaves of bread from the oven. It took us hours to kill the jumping fiends. My beautiful house is in shambles.

Our crops and food supply for this next winter, wiped out in a single afternoon! Our green world turned gray in a few short hours. I have never felt so utterly destitute. We spent the rest of the day walking around in shock, looking for a green blade of grass or some vegetation. It is all gone.

August 13

Last month's devastation is still on our minds, but we decided to go on with the meeting. Our growing community has decided to start a school. Neighbors met at the Robinson home to discuss their concerns. We elected officers to oversee the organization of School District #46. Benjamin Robinson is the director, Charles Wheaton the clerk, and Robert Wheeler, treasurer. We made plans for a school-house and pledged our support. It was a very tough decision, because every farm was damaged by the grasshoppers, but our children need schooling. Carl offered an acre of our land on the northeast corner as our contribution. This will put the school in the center of the district.

Until the school is built, the class of 16 pupils will be held in the Robinsons' home and taught by Miss Torey. They have two rooms, so one can be the school.

Adelaide was given the honor of the naming the school, because she has done so much for all the neighbors. She decided on the name "Lone Star," since it is the lone school this side of the Smoky Hill River.

September 24

News of the grasshopper devastation and plight of the people has spread throughout the nation. The Kansas Legislature has been too slow to get us help. We are living on eggs and what little we had left in the cellars. The chickens are the only animals that are well-fed because they can feast on the thousands of dead grasshoppers still laying around. The cows are not producing much milk now because they have nothing to eat. People from the Eastern states have sent food and clothing in a relief drive for the Plains states, but that is barely putting a dent in the help that we need in Kansas.

December 17

Our fourth child, Alfred, was born today. He is small because I haven't had enough to eat this fall. Alfred is blonde and, so far, very quiet. He has no idea what a hard road is ahead of him in this land.

This has been a bad winter for us, since most of our crops were devoured by the grasshoppers. We didn't harvest as much wheat and rye earlier in the year because of the drought.

The cellars are almost empty. Potatoes were the only crop we were able to harvest and store. There was no fruit to dry. Since we have no extra crops, we cannot trade for other supplies or food. This reminds me of the first years of drought in Sweden, but back then I didn't have four children to worry about. I pray that the grace of God will see us through.

December 25

We celebrated the birth of Jesus in a quiet way this year. No presents, special treats or church service. I am not up to traveling all the way to Salemsborg Church so soon after Alfred's birth. Carl read Bible stories to the children and told of our Christmas days in Sweden when we were young. Both sets of parents were over last night to wish us *God Jul.* Svärfar mentioned that the new Bethany Church was going to have its first service tomorrow. The congregation left the small church in the country and built a large stone church in Lindsborg. He cannot go see the new building now, because of leaving the church earlier this year, but I hope that in time they can attend a service there. They were good friends of Dr. and Mrs. Olsson. Our church and pastor are important. In times like these, we need our Lord for strength and endurance.

Pupils in front of the Lone Star School

1875

Lone Star School

January 25

It has been a terrible month, one blizzard after another. The temperature has been below zero many days. My fingers have gotten frostbite just carrying the milk pails from the barn to the house. The lack of food has left both the family and the livestock in poor shape. The drifts block the paths for the wagon trails and are big enough to stop the trains from delivering supplies to towns. The snowdrift in the edge of the corral is so packed and high that Blacky, our little pony, walked out over it and didn't sink in.

Bengt Hessler was here today with news. The southeast members presented a petition to the church board on January 18th asking to separate from Salemsborg Church. Our church is against us leaving, because it will split the congregation (and their money supply) almost in half. I wish they could understand that we like the pastor, but the church is too far for us to travel.

A resolution was passed by the Salemsborg congregation to urge the pastor to travel to the southeast district to preach on Sunday afternoons. We were not happy with this solution, because it still did not give us a church building to worship in.

Bengt also brought happy news that Olaf and Elsa had a daughter, named Gunilla, on the 22nd. This is Olaf's first child.

February 6

There were 117 people who said they would support the new church at a special meeting today. I hated to get the children out in this weather, but this was important.

We will submit a petition for admission to the Augustana Church Synod that meets on May 6th at Vasa, Minnesota. Olof Thorstenberg will go as our delegate. The biblical name "Assaria" was picked for the church's name. It means, "The Lord will help." We will need His help to convince the Synod to allow us to split from Salemsborg.

It's all worked out. If the petition is approved, the church dues will be $5 for married men and their families, $3 for the unmarried men and $2 for unmarried women. Since Pastor Dahlsten will be serving us, we will meet at three on Sunday afternoon in the summer and two during the winter.

The men of the neighborhood are almost done building the new school. They worked on it whenever they could. The lumber was hauled from Salina. It took a long time for the oxen and loaded wagons to cover the cross-country trails back to the school sight. The water was too high to ford the river so they had to go up north to the Iron Avenue bridge to get to Salina.

February 15

The ground was frozen and covered with snow, but the first grave has been dug in the new church cemetery. Eleven-year-old Thomas Olson died. He was coughing heavily during the meeting last week. I suppose he caught pneumonia. He and his family moved into the area recently. I had just met his mother at the last church meeting. I feel so sorry for her, being new to America with no family or friends for support. Next time Carl goes to town, I will send some bread with him to give the family. Our supplies are still low, but our spirits are higher than that poor family.

February 26

Tonight neighbors came by foot, horseback and lumber wagon to the school dedication festival. Every family in this area has sacrificed hard-earned money to buy the materials for the school. The building will also be used as the community hall for socials, meetings and Sunday school.

The frame building is 32 by16 feet. A large wooden star was fashioned and adorns the east side to show with pride that it is the Lone Star School. Mr. Amos Flumerfelt has been employed to teach the first three-month term. He will be paid $35 a month.

The committee held the very first oyster soup supper in this area. My kitchen was used to prepare the meal, since it is the closest house to the school. Kettles of milk and oysters (donated by the committee members) were simmered for the soup and the smell drifted through the whole house. The table was loaded with fresh-baked loaves of wheat bread and juicy fruit pies. With nearly 40 children in the district, you can imagine how many we had to feed when you count the siblings, parents, grandparents and every bachelor who wanted a free meal.

Everyone enjoyed the program of readings and singing. The old people smiled as they listened to the little ones recite their lines. The children had been working on the program during school at the Robinsons'. I think Mr. Lapsley sat in on some of their practices. He was beaming like he had taught the children himself. After the program he told them: "Now you learn good! You don't know what a privilege it is to get to go to school!"

Seven years ago I was a lonely young woman, standing in the tall grass on this very spot of land. I was homesick and yearned for neighbors to fill the gap caused by separation from my family and homeland. Now this corner holds a building bursting with family and friends.

March 1

The first day of school at Lone Star. I brushed Christina's hair, braided it and tied it with a pretty strip of calico. She wanted to wear the good heavy gingham dress that she usually wears for church. I said she could as a treat on her first day.

I'm glad we are close to the school. Some children will have to walk three or four miles.

When we walked Christina to school I wasn't surprised to see Mr. Lapsley greeting everyone in the schoolyard. He has taken a special interest in all the children's welfare. Since I had all three little ones along, Mr. Lapsley walked us home. He had Alfred in his arms as Willie rode "horseback" on him and I had Alma. The children giggled all the way.

I think Mr. Lapsley should get married and have children but he thinks a black woman wouldn't be welcome in the community. How sad that he feels that way.

April 26

Everyone has such high hopes for this year's crops after last year's disaster. Carl said that there are grasshoppers hatching out along the fence line. I noticed the chickens have been heading toward the field when I turn them out of their coop in the morning. Fresh grasshoppers are probably very tasty after this winter's slim pickings. The chickens are giving us eggs again. They quit laying last winter when it was so cold.

May 21

This morning we got our second shower for the week. It is so good to see green grass, flowers blooming and leaves on the trees. I won't take nature's beauty for granted this year. We have learned to get by on so little and not to waste anything. I guess this was God's way of making us appreciate what He has given us.

The new grasshoppers had been chewing on the first rows on the south edge of the corn field, but they disappeared when the rains started. We had to buy part of the garden seed, because I couldn't save any when the garden was destroyed. Our money reserve is now almost depleted. I pray we have a good harvest and fill the granary and cellars full.

June 27

Our brother-in-law Edvin is dead. Anna got word that her husband was killed while working on his railroad job. They buried his body out west instead of sending it back here. He had been working in western Kansas this summer, helping to lay the railroad tracks. The family really needed the money. She had been taking care of the children and homestead alone. Anna must deal with death for the fourth time. She will need our help and God's support.

September 29

It's a warm, mellow fall day. Weather like this makes me want to stay outside. Soon the winds will turn cold and the stove in the house will beckon me instead.

We finally got apples, peaches and cherries from our orchard. We dried most of the crop, but kept the best apples fresh to eat this winter. I made some applesauce and apple butter. We didn't have enough to squeeze for cider, but maybe next year.

We had so many pumpkins, we sliced and dried part of the crop to take up less room in the cellar. I gave the hogs the squash and pumpkins that had bad blemishes. My whole body sighed with relief when we got the garden harvested and stored for the winter. I have been been worried all summer that something would happen and we would not have enough to eat. I'm not sure we could handle another winter like the last one.

Hannah Carlson has returned to marry cousin Peter. Her father finally got his way. Peter and Hannah were wed today by Pastor Dahlsten. I don't think this is starting out as a happy marriage.

The Assaria Church committee has heard from the Salemsborg Church board. Even though the synod has refused our request to start a new church, the differences have been worked out. Assaria will become a daughter church to the one at Salemsborg. Pastor Dahlsten will serve us both. In the meantime, we will meet and worship at Salemsborg or a schoolhouse until our church can be built. Since Lone Star School is finished, Pastor will be encouraged to come to our community to hold church services.

December 25

We sang *"Hosianna"* with vigor this morning at *Julotta*. We have survived the year, our family is healthy and the future looks good. There is a reason for the trials God gives us. We must always remember that He will give us a shoulder to lean on when we are in despair.

The sky was just starting to show the pink glow of winter dawn as we came out of the church. What a good sign for the new year.

24. Hosianna!

"Hosianna" version from the Mission Friend's Song Book

1876

The Tornado

January 8

The Robinsons' baby was born today. They named him Nathan Thomas, after Adelaide's father, Nathan Smith. Adelaide's father and his wife, Cyrene, live near them, so she has help. I brought over a pie and a pot of stew. Benjamin is very happy tonight.

March 5

Willie is excited to start school tomorrow. From Christina he has picked up counting numbers, the alphabet and reading simple words. Since the school is close by, and Christina is old enough, I won't have to walk him to school. He was concerned about the pencil that Carl had given him last week. He was sure Albert was going to hide it or break it. I made *pepparkakor* for their school lunch for an extra treat for the first day.

March 16

With four growing children, our house has become too small. We had hoped to add on sooner, but it hasn't been possible until now. It is going to be an American two-story frame house.

I will have to move my flower bed from its place on the east side. I've collected wildflower seeds in the fall from the open prairie and now I have a beautiful variety of flowers around our home. Columbine and daisies bloom in the spring. I enjoy the primrose and phlox in the summer and the goldenrod and asters in the fall. The wild rose roots I dug up have spread everywhere so I have a nice stand of them. I throw my wash water on the flower beds when I empty the tubs, so they are well watered. I love the splash of color the flowers have added to the homestead. We dug up several small cedar and ash saplings from the riverbank and transplanted them around the house, but they are out far enough that they won't have to be moved.

We have bought lumber, glass for windows and doors to build on four rooms. We will add two rooms to the east part of the stone room, with two rooms directly above it. Since the cellar is already a nice size, we will not dig a basement for the new section.

Carl will put in a staircase to the upstairs and seal off the hole in the ceiling we have been using to get to the loft. We'll add a door to the side of the loft at the top of the stairway and use that area for an attic.

The southeast room will be our bedroom. A smaller bedroom to the north will be used as Alfred's nursery, and we'll have a storage closet under the stairwell. A stove in our room will heat the new section of the house.

At the top of the stairs will be one small room for Willie and a larger room to the south for the girls. The girls are excited about having their own room, away from their brother! The upstairs will be cold during the winter, but the children can come downstairs to dress in front of the kitchen stove.

The walls will be plastered and eventually papered. There is enough wood for trim inside around the windows, doors and baseboards. I'll need to make more curtains and Carl will have to make more furniture.

Carl even bought extra siding to cover the sandstone walls on the old part of the house. After we paint, the house will be done.

April 30

Moder came back home after being at Sara's this week. Sara had a little girl named Ida Josephina on the 26th. Both are doing fine.

May 9

Peter and Hannah have built a sod house this spring. It is much better than the small dugout he had built for himself when he homesteaded five years ago.

June 7

A tornado ripped a path from Lindsborg to Brookville today. We spent an hour in the cellar until we knew the storm had passed. We have headed to the cellar for other storms, but this was too close for comfort. We could all feel that a storm was brewing. The cows were restless and would not stand still to be milked, and Spot would not leave Carl's side. When Carl came in for forenoon coffee, we both stood on the front porch and watched the thunderhead building in the south. The morning had been windy, but when the wind died down suddenly and the birds stopped chirping, we knew things were changing for the worse. There were little bump-like baskets forming on the bottom of the storm cloud. When the sky turned yellow-green and the cloud bumps started to spin and pull downward, we grabbed the children and lunged toward the cellar door. Spot was with us, but the children were crying and worried about the other animals. I was worried about the house caving in on us, and Carl was worried about the buildings and crops. It sounded like there was a huge locomotive bearing down on us.

I don't know if the tornado actually touched down here, but we had minor damage to the granary. The wheat in the field was laid down in swirl patterns, like a giant hand put it's palm on the ground and twisted to the right. When we walked out to the garden, I couldn't figure why it looked different, but then I saw one of the cherry trees was gone! The wind twisted it off right at ground level and didn't even leave a stump. We found it 500 feet away. Even though the cherries were not quite ripe, we picked them off the downed tree. All the children could help, since the fruit was on their level for once. Overall, we were lucky not to have more damage than we did.

The longhorns being held at the river bend were spooked by the storm. They crossed the water and ran through several neighbors' farms. The cattle went right over dugouts, gardens and haystacks. Carl has gone to help with the roundup.

June 19

I received my naturalization papers today. I decided since Carl and the children were American citizens, I should become a citizen too. Instead of Maja Kajsa Swenson, I am now Mary C. Swanson. I don't know why I can't keep the name I was born with. I imagine the government thinks we should all have American names. My family will still call me Kajsa no matter what President Grant says.

July 4

Today is the centennial of the signing of the Declaration of Independence. I don't get so excited about the 4th of July, but the Robinsons do. They invited all of the neighbors over for a picnic at their homestead.

We heard some disturbing news at the picnic. General George Custer and 650 of his troops were massacred by the Indians near Little Big Horn, in Montana Territory on June 25th. A horse and a scout were the only Army survivors. The general patrolled Kansas back in the '60s when the first railroad was being built through western Kansas, so he has worked against the Indians for many years. I feel sorry for the soldiers who lost their lives and for the wives who must now be alone. But, I do not blame the Indians for wanting to defend their way of life and protect their families. They have suffered ever since the white man moved into Indian territory. I would fight to protect my children and farm too.

September 18

Sadly there is a new grave at the Assaria Church cemetery. Måns and Bothilda's 3-month-old daughter Mary died.

We have been stripping sorghum this week. It is a hard process to strip the leaves, cut and bundle the stalks and load them on the wagons. The stalks are crushed and then the green juice is boiled down to dark brown molasses. I hope to have several 15-gallon crocks full before we are done. Sorghum molasses is so good on buttermilk pancakes.

December 22

The fall has gone so quickly. Christmas is almost here and I'm not ready for it. I've had my hands full taking care of sick children. Alfred has recovered, but Willie still has a cough. Mr. Lapsley has been so worried about Willie that he brought over his favorite home remedy (turpentine and lard) to rub on Willie's chest. I think the visit did as much good as the smelly concoction.

1877

Gone in a Flash

January 28
We heard in church today that Olaf and Elsa had a second girl on the 25th. They named her Mathilda.

March 4
Rutherford Hayes is the new president of the United States. Besides changes in the White House, there will be changes in ours. I am going to have another child in November. Carl is hoping for another boy. I just hope it is healthy.

We have hired a man to help us with the farming this year. Carl wants to finish plowing the prairie land we have left for fields. Mabry is from back East and doesn't talk much. Carl fixed him a room in the granary. He will sleep there this summer, but he will eat meals with us.

March 6
We had a late snow storm this weekend, but it is melting fast. To take a break from being inside the house, I bundled up Alma and Alfred and we walked over to the schoolhouse at recess. There were snowballs flying as fast as the children could throw them. It looked like the girls' side was winning though. They were more cautious in taking aim and were hitting their opponents instead of flinging snowballs wildly in the air like the boys were doing. I'm sure the teacher hates to clean the floor after the children have been out in the mud and snow, but it gives her a moment's peace, and it lets the children work off steam.

May 13

Anna has remarried, this time to Ola Peterson, Måns' younger brother. We had them over for a meal today and I served fish that the children caught from the river. That reminded Ola of a story about one of their first Christmas dinners when his family moved to Kansas. I remember when it happened because that was the talk at *Julotta* that year. We only had Christina then, so our children hadn't heard the story.

Ola told that on that evening, the family was eating their *Julafton smörgåsbord* when a band of Indians broke into the house, intending to raid their meal. One Indian scooped a big spoonful of hot mustard sauce into his mouth, not realizing what it was. He thought the sauce had set his mouth on fire. With tears running down his cheeks, he choked and spun around the room, spitting out the sauce. The family was afraid they would all be scalped on the spot. Unable to speak to the Indians in their words, Ola put just a dab of the mustard sauce on a piece of *lutfisk* and ate it to show the Indian that the sauce must be used sparingly. Ola's quick thinking spared the family, but the Indians still dumped the platters of food into their leather bags to take with them. They did not take the bowl of mustard sauce though!

May 19

The Assaria Church construction has started. It will be a wooden frame building, with an entry way facing the south. Some day we hope to add a steeple to the top of the entry, with a bell to ring God's glory throughout the countryside on Sunday mornings.

June 15

Carl surprised me with a birthday present this morning. Last time he was in town he bought a jewelry pin for me. It is an oval black stone, set in an ornate gold backing. This is the first piece of jewelry he has given me since my wedding ring. Every time I put my hand to my throat and touch the pin I smile and think of my husband's thoughtfulness.

July 24

Carl is dead. He was killed on the 17th.

My mind is still numb. I have been in a state of shock all week. The day keeps playing over and over in my head. Maybe if I write down what happened, my mind will give me some peace.

Storm clouds were building in the west. Carl and Mabry were shocking the patch of oats left in the north field.

As it started to rain, more and more heavily, I thought how the men caught in the field would be soaking wet and disappointed if they didn't get done.

The noisy storm lasted quite a while. One crack of lightning came so close that it made the hair on the back of my neck stand up. I looked out the north kitchen window hoping it had not hit the schoolhouse.

When the men did not return home, I started to worry. Out the window I saw Svärmor running toward our house. I remember saying to the girls, "Something must be wrong, if Svärmor is coming. She rarely comes over."

I rushed outside and met her in the garden as she cut across the pumpkin patch, not even noticing she was tripping over the vines.

"Lightning hit them! Mabry was carrying the pitchfork on his shoulder and the lightning killed them both!" she screamed. "Johan found them on the road! My son is dead!"

As her words sank in, I fell to my knees, as if lightning had hit my soul. I didn't want to believe it. When their burned bodies were brought into the house, I fainted. Mabry was charred black.

The children were in shock. Christina screamed and screamed until she was exhausted. I wanted the children to go to Moder's, but they would not leave my side.

Johan rode over to get my parents. Moder was worried that the shock would harm me and the unborn child. I could not control my sobbing. I was so numb I could not feel the life within me.

The storm flooded the creek and river so we could not get to Assaria to give Carl a proper church burial. I wanted to wait, but it's so hot this time of the year. Andrew kindly suggested burying them on the hill in his pasture.

Svärfar, Johan and Emanuel built the casket for Carl. They put a piece of glass over the top, like a window, then the lid over that.

My brothers made Mabry's wooden casket. They didn't have any black paint for it, so they mixed turpentine and stove soot together to darken the wood. We didn't know who or where Mabry's next of kin were to notify them. He never talked about a family.

As I stood by the open graves, trying to listen to the final words spoken for the burials, my mind wandered back to the day we first moved here. Carl and I were young and healthy, ready to break the sod and build a family. We had such high hopes and dreams for our life on this prairie. And now, because of one bolt of lightning, I am a widow, with a farm and four children to take care of, and a baby due in November.

I am too scared and sad to stay home alone at night with the children. After supper, when the sun starts to set in the west, we walk down to Erick's house to spend the night. Carl is laid to rest only a quarter of a mile farther, but I will never be able to reach out to him again.

July 31

Mr. Lapsley brought over four kittens today, with the excuse he "found these animals" and didn't have any room or milk for them. I know he brought the kittens to give the children something to hug and talk to since they are so sad. He has been over twice a week to help with the chores and check in on us.

October 13

The world seems to stop when someone you love dies, but life keeps going, changing every day. I have to keep going, but it is so hard. My children have needed my constant love and reassurance that I am not going to leave them too. The corn crop still needs to be harvested. We planted more corn this year, since we had Mabry to help plant and harvest. Now, neither Carl nor Mabry is here to help me. My family and Mr. Lapsley have gotten the garden harvested and stored in the cellars. In my condition, I haven't been much help.

October 16

Bless the neighbors! I could not figure out what all the wagons were doing coming into the yard this morning. The whole neighborhood gathered today to harvest our corn. I just sat down on the porch and cried. No one said who, but I think Mr. Lapsley went around and arranged the day.

The men divided up in teams and made a race out of who could pick the most corn. As the wagons were filled, they came back to the granary, unloaded and headed back to the field.

Adelaide and Cyrene arrived shortly after the men, with food enough for the whole crew. I was still so shocked by all the help that I hadn't thought about how I was going to feed everyone at noon. They sat me down in the rocker that Carl had made for me and took over the kitchen. These two women fed 27 men in three shifts.

In one long day, they harvested what would have taken Carl and Mabry a month to do. I could not thank them enough for their help and support.

November 18

Our daughter Carolina was born today. I should be happy that she is a healthy baby, but I'm so sad that Carl isn't here to hold her. I've cried until I shouldn't have any tears left. Moder has taken Alma and Alfred to her house for a few days. Erick is helping Willie with the chores, and Christina is taking care of the baby and me.

Why did Carl have to die so young?

December 24

I could not put up the *ljus krona* this year. Ours has six branches on it. We started out with three branches when Carl first carved it, then added another each time we had a baby. When a family member dies you are supposed to take his branch off of the *ljus krona*, but I could not bring myself to take off Carl's branch. Besides, I did not have any presents to put under the tree for the children. I have been so exhausted by the strain of his death, farm work and the new baby that I put Christmas out of my mind.

We should be at the Assaria Church in the morning. It will be the first *Julotta* in our new church building. But I do not feel like celebrating Jesus' birth after God took away my Carl.

December 25

Christina brought the *ljus krona* down from the attic last night without me knowing it. Under the tree were two presents. One had a little note saying, "To Momma, with love from all your children." Inside the wrapping paper was a handkerchief that Christina had embroidered my initials on. The other package said "To Carrie, from

Poppa." I just stared at it for the longest time. The crying of the baby pulled me out of my trance. After I changed her and she had nursed, I held her sitting up in my lap and I opened her present. It was a little doll. It had a wooden head and a cloth body like the dolls Carl and I had made for our other girls. The scrap of dress had been sewn by young fingers. Carl must have carved the doll head last spring when I found out I was pregnant. Apparently Christina found it and made the body and dress for it.

I must have sat in the rocker for an hour, holding my little angel who had drifted back to sleep. When I heard the children stirring upstairs, I put Carolina back in her cradle and lit the candles on the *ljus krona*. Instead of Carl's branch, it is now Carolina's.

1878

The Hired Man

January 20

I don't know how much time I will have to write in my journal this year, but it helps to write down what I am feeling. I can't talk to the children about my loneliness.

More deaths among our neighbors and friends keep reminding me of my own loss. Bengt and Nellie Hessler lost their son Nathaniel to croup on December 30th.

Also, I have spent the week comforting Adelaide. Little Nathan died on the 15th. Instead of burying him at Assaria, he was buried on their land beside Luke, their other son. Adelaide is sick with grief.

March 3

Since it was a warm sunny morning, Erick insisted I dress up the children and go to church with him for Sunday services. I was beginning to relax and enjoy getting off of the farm until we went by the cemetery. There was another little grave on Måns Peterson's plot. We found out after church that little Esther died February 27th. Why does God punish us like this?

March 21

The hired man I needed has arrived. My prayers have been answered. I can't handle five children and run the entire farm by myself. They are old enough to be a big help, and my family pitches in, but I need a man to do the heavy work.

The feeding chores alone take up a good part of the morning and evening. We have acquired the usual assortment of farm animals over the past 10 years. Besides the teams of oxen and horses, we have cattle, hogs and a few sheep. The chickens and turkeys wander around the homestead during the day, but roost in the chicken house at night.

Mr. Peter Runeberg walked here all the way from Ford County, Illinois, this spring. Peter, his parents, six brothers and two sisters came to America in '71. He was 17 when they left Ysane, Sweden. He heard there was a large Swedish settlement in the Smoky River Valley in Kansas, with land still available for farming. Since most of the land was taken in Illinois, he took off to find some of his own. He needs a job while he is looking over this area.

May 18

I have kept Peter very busy with chores this spring. Many jobs were neglected after Carl died. Repairs needed to be done on equipment and harnesses, and the buildings needed to be cleaned out before the wheat crop could be harvested and stored.

Carl had broken the prairie to the south and north of the buildings so the fields now must be worked and planted. Since the creek occasionally floods, we have left the west part of the farm for pasture and the hay field.

July 6

Emma married Magnus Fager's son Frank today. It is good to see them together and happy. When they first announced their engagement I was jealous that she would be a blushing bride with a man at her side. I was just feeling sorry for myself because I am a widow. Moder and Fader had the wedding supper at their house.

July 17

Carl was killed one year ago today. We all remembered him in our thoughts and prayers.

September 12

Anna gave birth to triplets today. I wasn't surprised when two babies were born, but three! She'll have her hands full. The family and neighbors will take turns bringing meals to them for a while. Her older children are 8, 6 and 4, so they will be of some help with the babies. Ola is still in shock. They just got married and now he's the father of three girls!

September 21

All the family traveled to Assaria Church today for the baptizing of my three nieces. They were named Selma Elvira, Hilma Carolina and Ida Wilhelmina. They look so much alike I don't know how Anna is telling them apart. Thilda Svenson and I were the girls' sponsors.

October 13

A sad day for Anna and Ola. They buried little Selma and Hilma today. The girls caught cold on the way home from their baptism, and Selma and Hilma died, probably from diphtheria or pneumonia. For some reason Ida didn't catch the death of her sisters. Instead of going back to the church cemetery, the girls were buried beside their Uncle Carl, in Andrew's pasture. The men folk piled stones on top of the graves so the animals won't dig them up. I wonder if Carl knows he has two little nieces beside him to protect. Anna has lost five children and a husband. That is too much for a heart to bear.

October 30

Carl's sister Clara and her husband, Otto, have a new daughter. They named her Selma, in memory of Anna's lost daughter. Clara and Otto's 5-year-old son, August, died earlier this year.

November 19

Peter Olson has built a one-room frame house, only 6 by 8 feet, but Hannah said it was one of the happiest days of her life to move out of the ground and into that house. I assume they will be adding on as soon as possible.

Peter Runeberg has turned out to be a good hired man. Still, I hate to see him in the distance with the team of horses and plow. It reminds me of Carl plowing our first fields and the dreams he had for our farm.

December 10

Carrie is starting to toddle from chair to chair. We have to watch her around the stoves. She has not learned the word "hot" yet. Peter holds her after supper while I clean the kitchen and the girls wash the dishes. He helps the children with their spelling and geography lessons in the evenings.

Tonight during supper the children and I were talking about what we were going to prepare for our Christmas dinner. We knew we would have *lutfisk* and *potatiskorv*, but Alma was wanting to try something different too. Peter, who had been silently eating his meal, spoke up at Alma's question. He asked me to make a dish that his mother always makes for Christmas. His mother makes a *risan pudding* with *kräm*. He said it is made with rice, cream, eggs and sugar, but she adds ground cinnamon to it that makes it different. I started to say I was out of cinnamon when he reached into his coat pocket and pulled out a piece of cinnamon bark. When he went to town for the *lutfisk* last week, he bought cinnamon, but had not gotten up the nerve to ask me to make the special dish.

December 31

Peter shot and dressed two pheasants for our New Year's Eve dinner. He is full of surprises. He made us all little presents for Christmas.

It is strange to have a man at the meal table again, to wash his clothes and to have him sleeping in the house. But as I get to know him, I sleep easier at nights knowing I have help on the farm.

1879

New Towns

February 15
Claus and Sara lost their new baby yesterday. When Wilhelmina Carolina was born over 2 weeks ago, I was afraid she wouldn't last long. She wasn't healthy from the start. I wish the baby hadn't died on Oskar's 6th birthday though.

March 22
We are getting our mail at the new Bridgeport Post Office now. (The village on the river has been named Bridgeport because of the iron bridge.) That is so much more handy than going all the way to Salina. I enjoy reading the weekly *Svenska Härolden*, Salina's Swedish newspaper, that we get in the mail. The older children walk to Bridgeport to get the mail on Saturday, if Peter hasn't picked it up during the week while he is in town for supplies.

May 30
We heard that Olaf and Elsa Hessler had their third child yesterday, a girl named Emmy.

I spent part of the day dyeing the wool we sheared from our sheep this spring. I dyed part of the wool brown, boiling walnut husks to get the color I wanted. Tomorrow, I am going to dye a batch red, using red onion skins.

Alma presented me with a hand bouquet of wildflowers she had picked in the meadow. They were wilting by the time she wandered back to the house, but we put them in a jar of water to perk them up.

She just loves flowers and can spend hours working on her little flower patch by the well.

June 4

Highland Fairchild's land to the south of our church has been surveyed and laid out for the town of Assaria. The Kansas Pacific Railroad is building a line through the new town and putting in a depot.

July 8

Lindsborg has been incorporated into a town. Almost all of the 500 people that live there are Swedish. Because the railroad was built through Lindsborg this year, the town has boomed. Main Street businesses are multiplying. A bookstore, a hardware store, a lumber company, a tailor shop and a brickyard have started since we were last in town. The first English newspaper, *The Lindsborg Localist*, is being published by William McClintock. John Anderson built a grain elevator on the west side of the railroad tracks. That will be a great boost for the farmers to get their grain to market.

Bethany Church finally received its new pastor this month. The congregation has been without a formal leader since Dr. Olsson left in '77. Dr. Carl Swensson is a newly ordained minister and graduate of the Augustana College in Illinois. He was hand-picked by Dr. Olsson to lead the Bethany Church congregation.

It has turned hot. I'm glad I have a deep well to store my butter and meat in during the summer. The crocks and pails are suspended by rope into the cool, dark depths of the well. When I need the food, I just pull up the crock.

August 19

Måns and Bothilda lost their son Alfred today on his first birthday. Sometimes I dream about Carl and his death after I've heard that someone has died in the community. The hurt has faded, but I can still see the burned bodies of Carl and Mabry clearly in my mind.

September 21

I caught up on the news of the community this morning when we visited after church.

The worst news was that Nellie Hessler, Bengt's wife, died from consumption this week. She had been poorly for quite some time.

The Oban Post Office, that served the area around the church, has been renamed the Assaria Post Office, because that is what the railroad depot and the new town are called.

Svärfar told us today that he sold his 80 acres to Ola and Anna. I think Carl's parents will still live there, but Ola will farm the land.

November 21

We have a problem with mice. I have not had them in the house before, but there must be a nest of them somewhere. The tallow candles we made yesterday have been chewed on. I left them lying on the kitchen table last night. I will let one of the cats sleep in the house the rest of this week to see if we can't solve this problem.

December 13

Hannah Olson gave birth to her second daughter yesterday. They named her Alma Christina. My girls were thrilled that they have a namesake and Hilda, their first girl, is a proud big sister.

We enjoyed the Lone Star School Christmas program this evening. Christina and Willie gave presentations and Alma said a poem. Since there is such a large enrollment, the schoolhouse was packed with family and neighbors. We ended the evening with pie and coffee.

December 31

We heard there was a big prairie fire by Lindsborg today that burned several sections of land. It is unusual to get a fire at this time of year. Either a train started it, or someone was careless with his campfire.

1880

Butter in the Well

March 31

I haven't written in my journal this spring. Peter and I have been busy planting the crops and garden. I have taken my turn following behind the plow when other jobs arise that he needs to do instead. We seem to work well together.

May 23

After church today we drove over to Claus and Sara's to see the new twins. Emma Christina and Carl Emil were born on the 15th. They are tiny, but doing okay.

June 21

The threshing crew started on our wheat today. We have been busy making bread and pies to feed 12 extra people. This morning I started to pull the butter crock out of the well and the rope broke! It caught me by surprise and I fell on my rear end when the weight of the crock was suddenly gone. I hate to lose a crock like that, and there is just no way to retrieve the butter from the bottom of the well. There was not time to churn more before the meal. I was embarrassed when there was not enough butter for the men to spread on their bread at noon. Alma blurted the whole story to the crew and they had a good laugh.

One of the topics around the dinner table, besides my misfortune, was the new gallery and bell tower that have been added on to Bethany Church. Someone said a pipe organ will be installed soon. I want to go hear it some Sunday.

June 17

Peter Olson's little house became very crowded today. Peter's parents, Olof and Kajsa Bryngelson, and his sisters, Magdalena and Cathrina, moved in with them. Peter had saved up enough money to send for his family in Sweden. Their friend, Maria Petersson, came with them as well.

July 5

The Bridgeport mill has been rebuilt this year and they have added fine screens for white flour. We hauled part of our wheat there to be ground today. The miller keeps one-sixth of the flour in payment for the grinding. He sells the flour (under the name White Oak Flour) to people who don't have their own wheat to grind. This is so much handier than when we had to do it ourselves or go all the way to Salina.

July 27

All of the children have special chores to do during the summer. Alfred churns butter and gathers eggs. Alma delegates herself to the garden. Willie helps with the field work and Christina does the house cleaning. She always has the dust cloth in her hand.

Carrie, at 3, tries to spend most of her day playing with the animals. Spot is usually with her, so I don't have to worry if she gets out of my sight. Carrie usually has her arm wrapped around a cat's neck, dragging it around with her as she explores the farm yard.

August 13

Since the school enrollment has grown so much over the last few years, the east section of our district is going to build its own schoolhouse three miles to the east. The new school in District #59 will be Wheeler School, named after Robert Wheeler, who donated the land. We are dropping the "Lone" from "Lone Star School" since it is not the only school in the district anymore. Alfred will start school this year so Carrie will be my only child left at home. Children grow up so fast.

September 13

Anna and Ola had a daughter, Lovinia Hildegard, today. She is healthy, but Anna is exhausted. I went over to help her and fix meals for the family. Ola likes my watermelon rind pickles, so I brought a small crock along for him.

September 28

The cellar is well-stocked this year. Besides carrots, potatoes, turnips, pumpkins and winter squash, we finally got a good crop from the apple and pear trees. All summer the girls and I have made jams, pickles and tomato preserves. We canned corn, beans and beets. I have three crocks of cabbage in brine down in the cellar. After the frost hits the garden, we will harvest the dry beans.

It makes me feel good to see all of the jars lined up on the shelves. So many shapes and sizes, filled with hues of yellow, red and green.

October 15

The neighbor ladies met at my house today to help me quilt. This quilt has a variety of pieces of material from old dresses and coats. It is the crazy quilt pattern and we are embroidering different types of stitches around each piece using red, green and yellow threads. Peter needs a new quilt for his bed, and I thought this pattern would be more masculine. He helps me so much here that I want to do something nice for him.

Svärmor could not come today because she is helping at Clara and Otto's this week. Their newest daughter, Beda, was born on the 12th.

November 28

We had a big crowd for church today. Christina sang in the choir. The church board gave us a report after church. We are trying to get our own pastor so Pastor Dahlsten does not have to split his time between us and Salemsborg. So far we have called five pastors and four have declined.

December 12

After church today we rode over to Claus and Sara's to give them their Christmas basket. A red-eyed Claus met us at the door. Sara was inside rocking Carl, who had just died.

The family in front of the homestead

1881

Drought and Death

March 4

James Garfield has been inaugurated as the newest president of the United States.

This was fine for the country, but we will remember this day as the day we lost Spot. He died of old age. Peter buried him under the cedar tree north of the house. We will all miss him.

March 28

Andrew married Maria Petersson today in Salina. Jonathan Weaver, the probate judge of Saline County, performed the ceremony. We had the wedding supper at our house when they got home from town.

We got a new puppy from Erick Carlson's litter of pups, so the children had fun playing with it. Alfred named the puppy Rusty, for the color of his hair.

May 5

A photographist stopped by to ask if I would like a picture taken of us and the farm. He has been traveling around the area this week. I decided it would be a good idea because we do not have such a picture. Carl and I had talked about it, but we never found the time or money.

We brought the animals out of the barn to show how well we are doing. We stood in front of the house. I asked Peter to be in the picture also, since he helps us out so much.

July 3

Peter and Hannah's first child, Hilda, died yesterday at age 3. She was buried at the Assaria cemetery. When we were standing in the graveyard I noticed several new graves. Summer complaint has taken the lives of many young children.

We heard more sad news while at Assaria. President Garfield was shot yesterday at a railroad station in Washington, D.C. So far the president is hanging on. The man who shot him, a Charles Guiteau, was arrested on the spot. He said that "God ordered him to kill the president." Guiteau apparently bought a special gun to shoot the president because he thought the gun would be attractive in a museum. I believe the poor man is insane.

One note on the bright side was that Olaf and Elsa had a healthy new son early this morning. They named him Perry Leonard.

August 24

Peter Olson had another death today. His sister Cathrina died of consumption. She was 26.

It has been a drought year. The hot winds withered the crops away. We had thunderclouds, but they never developed into rain showers. Wheat harvest was hard work for very little grain. The crop was short and the heads were not filled out. We will get a poor yield on the corn and sorghum too. We have worked hard days without much to show for it.

September 21

The president died two days ago from blood poisoning. There were complications from the gunshot wounds he received in July. Vice-President Chester Arthur will take over his post.

October 15

Bethany Church has started the Bethany College. This year the students and one professor are meeting at the pastor's study at church.

October 24

A fourth grave at Måns Peterson's plot. Alfred was almost 11 months old. He was named after the son they lost in '79. Now they are buried together. The churchyard is being filled with little graves. Children have such a harsh life stuck out on the homestead. When they come down with a disease there is no doctor to help them.

December 24

A day of gloom for us. Rusty was killed this morning. He had been chasing the wagons as they went by the farm. Today he misjudged a team's speed and was run over by the horses and wagon. We buried Rusty beside Spot.

This has been a hard year for everyone in the neighborhood. Drought and disease have taken their toll. It will be a sad Christmas.

1882

Losing my Parents

January 10

Moder died yesterday. She was 71. I felt so torn to leave her in the cold ground and walk away. The frozen ground made it hard for the men to dig the grave. When Fader and I prepared her for the coffin, I insisted we put on her best cloak and woolen mittens. Fader said she will be warm in heaven tonight.

I will miss her deeply, but I am so grateful that we were reunited in Kansas before her time came to depart from this earth. Peter has been a great comfort to me this week.

March 29

We heard Handel's "Messiah" sung at the Salemsborg Church today. A group of Lindsborg people, lead by Alma Swensson (wife of the Bethany Church pastor), gave the performance to raise money for the Bethany College building fund. They had been practicing since December and were very good. They sang at Bethany Church yesterday.

March 31

Willie Lamkin died today. It was so hard to explain to my son Willie that his classmate is dead. The Lamkins also lost an infant son in February.

June 1

Charles Gunnerson is building a grain elevator on the east side of the railroad tracks in Lindsborg. It is a joint stock company made up of local farmers, so it will be called the Farmers Elevator.

October 10

Fader is dead. In some ways I am relieved that he is with Moder. He was so lonely without her. I think that hastened his death. My brothers and I spent the day reminiscing about Sweden, when we were young and our parents were strong and healthy.

I took a good look at myself in the mirror tonight when I was getting ready for bed. My face is weather-beaten and leathery from working outside all year round. My hands are red and chapped from washing and work. I had not thought of myself as aging until Moder died. I have not felt well this year. I believe mourning has taken its toll.

December 7

I gave Christina a gold watch for her 16th birthday. It is the custom for the father to give the watch to the child, but Carl is gone. She is growing up strong. (She is taller than I am now.) He would have been proud of her.

We finally had a pastor accept the call to our church. Pastor A.M. LeVeau will be serving our congregation next year.

December 25

It has been a difficult Christmas without my parents. I feel so old now that they are gone. I will be the next generation to age and die. Dawn was rising over the cemetery when we came out of the church after *Julotta*. I walked across the snow in the silent graveyard to tell Moder and Fader *"God Jul."*

1883

Marrying Again

January 16

Andrew came over to get me early this morning to help Maria with her childbirth. She had a daughter—Carolina Josefina Emelia. I wish Moder could have seen her. The baby reminds me of Emma when she was a baby.

Erick rented out our parents' house to Tom Olson. I hate to see someone else live in Moder's house, but we don't want it to stand vacant.

April 13

Erick and Magdalena Olson were married today by Pastor Le-Veau at the Assaria parsonage. We had the wedding supper at my house. They waited a long to time get married. Erick is 45 and Magdalena is 32. They have known each other since we were cousins growing up together in Sweden. When Magdalena came to America, she worked in the broomcorn fields around Freemont and New Gottland and was a hired girl for a family in Smolan.

Pastor told them that Bengt Hessler is getting remarried—to Hannah Swenson—tomorrow.

As we were clearing the table, Erick was teasing Magdalena, saying that he didn't want any of their bread made on the dirt floor of their house. She turned beet red, explaining that the family in Smolan who she worked for were English, and of course she had some problems understanding them. She thought the mistress instructed her "to put the newly baked bread on the *floor*," so she did.

The woman was talking about rolling the bread dough to be baked in *flour*, but the translation came out mixed.

May 6

Christina was confirmed today at Assaria Church. She received a new Bible from the congregation. We celebrated with a family dinner at our home.

Erick is building on a frame addition to his house, three rooms downstairs and a half-story upstairs. Andrew and Peter have been helping him.

May 28

Claus and Sara's new daughter, Selma Secelia, was born yesterday. Emma went over to help with the children and cooking for a week. We will all go to visit when Selma is baptized at the Mission Friend's Church.

August 24

Carl's brother Emanuel was over today telling us that Johan got caught in that bad hailstorm that was south of us yesterday. Johan and Eva Swenson are building a stone house on land just north of Andrew's farm. They don't have enough money for lumber for a frame house, so Johan has been digging stones to use. Johan had the team hitched to the wagon yesterday morning to go get another load of stone. Emanuel told Johan he thought it was going to storm, but Johan said a little rain wouldn't stop him. Johan got halfway to where he was going and it started to rain, then it turned to hail the size of two fists placed together. He unhitched the horse, crawled under the wagon and pulled the horse's head under the wagon bed. The force of the hail stones bruised the poor horse and took the hair off its hide. Johan came home without the stone, but glad to be alive.

September 6

I got a letter today from Carl's sister Sara Lisa, who lives in Ackley, Iowa. Their ninth child was born on August 19th.

Closer to home, Bridgeport has been growing in leaps and bounds, ever since the Southwest Railroad built a depot there. The Peck Cheese Factory is expanding and buying milk from area farmers. I'm happy the hotel has added a drugstore in their building, but I was bothered to hear that one of the general stores is adding a saloon.

December 21

The "widow Swenson" became Mrs. Peter Runeberg today. We were married by Pastor LeVeau at the parsonage in Assaria. Since we've been sharing the farm and our lives for five years, we decided to get married. We had a wedding meal at Magnus Fager's house afterward. Since the whole family was going to be there, we decided to hire a photographist to take our picture.

Carrie cornered Mr. Fager to ask him about her "real father," since Magnus knew him well. Even though Peter raised her, she is driven to find out about her father. I believe it is because people know that she was the baby born after her father was killed by lightning. I wish she hadn't brought up the subject today.

I thought of my first wedding, almost 18 years ago. What would life be like today if Carl was still alive?

Family gathering at the Fager home

40.59	40.89	40	14	40.80	40.70	40.60	4051	4082	41.01	4192

Swan Stifft

John A.

Salemsburg P.O. 40.90

C   O   P.J.   A.   Carl

L.P. Nelson 40   32.20

Ahleen 80   6

Salemsburg Church 80

Nelson 80   5

W.nson 40   Norquist 40   Fehr 40   4

J.P. Carlson 200   32.28

Res.

S.E. Johnson 160

80

80

J.P. Lofgreen 80

F O Nelson 96   32.36

C.V. Rosberg

A. Johnson

J.A. 79 School No 37

A. 80

80 A.J.

P R bloom 80   32.57   32.93

C.V. Rosberg 160   7

Res.

C.J. Lindholm 80   8

Applequist 160

Sandberg 80

C.J. Lindholm 80

Thelander 80

L.M. Thelander 80   9

Gust. Lindholm 80   33.21

Res.

S. A 80

N M 80

A.V. Anderson Res 80

F.A. Ecklund 80

S.A. Miller 320

Hammer 80   33.78   33.72

BUTTES

S.A. Holt 160   18

Johnson 80

A.T. Sniggs 80   17

S.F. Johnson 160

A.P. Swanson 160   16

Res H Hanson 160

J.G.Pet 80

Johnes 33.65   O Nelson   33.65

Bengston 120

P W Swanson 120

S.A. Holt 80

A. Abrahamson 160

Emil 80 Wernlof

John Lusell 160

Nels Bmstrom 80   35.14   33.04

C.Johnson 160   19

P.J. Tengloff 80

80

V. Olson 80   20

A E Van Loon 160

Ang. Erick 160   21

Chas Viberg 80   34.12   34.62

N.G. Nelson 160

J.A. Brattstrom 80

Harding 80

Jonas Johnson 80

John Johnson 80

J. Elmquist 160

Erickson 160

Olson 80   34.91   34.25

J Peterson 80

80   40

40

A E. VanLoon 80

F. Helm 160

Jno. Carlson 80

C. Carlson 80

Anna Axelson 80

28

Sanstrom 40   35.03   C Carlson 40   35.69   30

A. Anderson 80

Nils Anderson 80

Brand & Nolander 160

School No 38

G. Magnusson 160

P Backman 80

L.J. Larson 80

Swan Anderson 80

J.A. Pihl 80

Res E.M. Berglund 80   35.26   35.87

O. Lindquist 160   31

G. Engberg 160

G. Johnson 160   32

C Brand 106⅔

A.P. Brand 106⅔   33

Mission Church

A. Brand 106⅔

E.M. Anderson Res 80

A.G. Magnusson 160

Fred Hjerpe 80

E.M. Anderson Res 80

John Bjorn 160

C.P. Warholm 80

A. Aden 80

G. Lindberg 120

A. Jacobson 40

1884-Saline County, Kansas

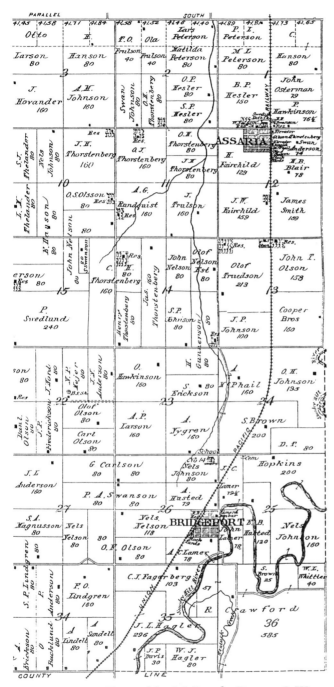

Township 16 South. Range 3 West.

1884-Saline County, Kansas

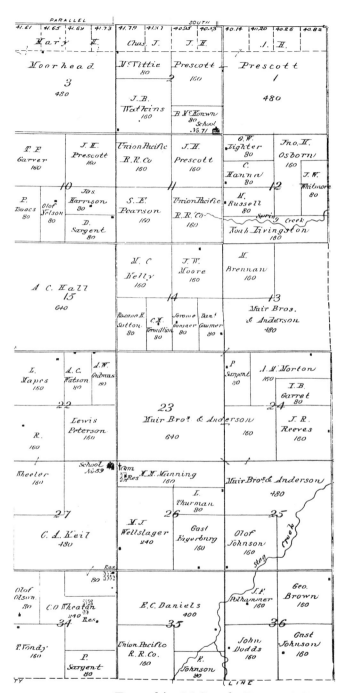

Township 16 South. Range 2 West.

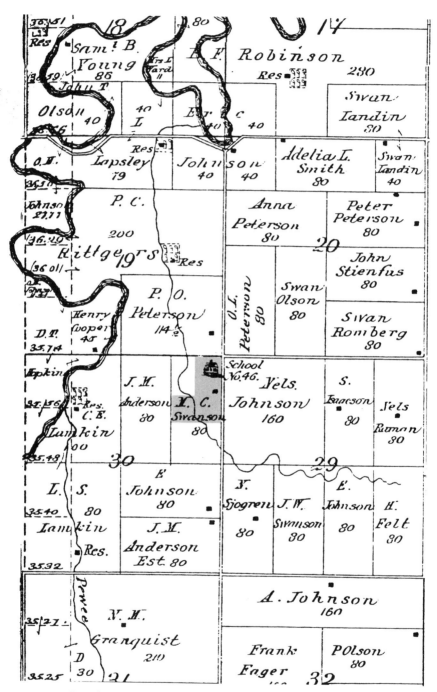

Portion of Township 16 South. Range 2 West.

104

1884

Julia Linnea

January 27

Our Salemsborg friends, Samuel and Christina Johnson, lost two children to consumption this week. Eight-year-old Theodore died on the 18th, and 4-year-old Almeda the next day. They have lost four children. I remember when their Axel and Phena died shortly after they came from Sweden. Consumption is a disease that parents dread because few children survive.

With death comes new life. Erick and Magdalena's first child, Carolina Emelia, was born the 26th. And, I will be having another child this summer.

April 6

All of the family gathered today at Assaria Church for Willie's confirmation. When visiting after church we heard there had been a prairie fire in western Kansas that scorched seven counties. With the strong winds we get in this state, I can see why the fire kept spreading.

Peter and Hannah have sold the homestead and moved to Assaria. They are going to run the livery stable with Hannah's brother, Olof Carlson. Peter is very good with horses, but I don't know if he is going to like living in town. He likes the country life. Hannah was happy to be in town when their daughter, Emma Otelia, was born yesterday. Assaria's new doctor assisted in the delivery.

June 21

Olaf Hessler died today. He leaves Elsa with six children. Their newest child, Odelia, was born just six weeks ago.

July 2

I gave birth to our daughter, Julia Linnea, today. I chose the middle name for the flowers I remember in Sweden. She has Peter's round face and dark hair. The older children had been teasing me that it would be a Fourth of July baby. Carl's children range in age from 7 to 17, and are growing up so fast. It will be fun to have a baby around again.

August 11

Peter brought home another load of lumber from Assaria today. We are going to add on to the house again. The new rooms, tacked on to the northeast, will give us more space upstairs and downstairs.

The new room off of the kitchen will become our bedroom so our old room can be a parlor. We need a room to receive our guests, especially now that the children are having friends over. Lace curtains and wallpaper would dress up the room. And we will need a loveseat and chairs. I also want to get a piano so the girls will learn music.

The upstairs addition will be one big room for Willie and Alfred. Christina, Alma and Carrie will share the south upstairs bedroom and Julia will be in the little room downstairs. The Star School teacher would like to board with us, since we are close to the school. She could use the little bedroom upstairs.

It seems like every time the family grows, we need to shift rooms.

September 2

Bridgeport has divided its school district. A new schoolhouse is being built in town and the District #14 school that was on the north end of town will be moved to a site one mile north.

The townspeople have built a park just west of the bridge and poplar trees line the streets. The town will soon rival Salina at the rate it is growing.

December 25

It has been a happy, busy Christmas season. We baked dozens of cookies and breads. Each child has a favorite that we had to make. Besides what we wanted for company, we needed cookies for the children's school program, the neighbors' baskets and plenty to nibble on ourselves.

The children had a lot of fun making presents for one another. I came across hidden presents from the attic to the cellar until we put up the *ljus krona*.

The children went caroling and to several sledding parties in the neighborhood. Last Sunday, Peter and I delivered Christmas baskets to neighbors.

The spirit of Christmas has been in all of us this year and we have thoroughly enjoyed the season.

Assaria Lutheran Church

1885

Community Socials

March 4

Grover Cleveland has become the 22nd president of the United States. Peter heard about the inauguration at the general store in Bridgeport when he took a crate of eggs in to sell.

April 6

I got an oleander plant for the parlor last week. Most of the year it is a green bushy plant, but it blooms clusters of bright pink flowers in the summer. I was told to put it in the cellar during the winter so it will go dormant, but to open the cellar door when the weather is sunny to give it winter light. I put it in the southwest corner of the room, right by the piano. It added the finishing touch to the parlor.

After the Easter service yesterday, the family came to our house for the afternoon. The girls played the piano for the women in the parlor, and the men sat out on the porch and visited. Seems like we always end up in separate rooms.

August 9

The English-speaking neighbors have been holding Sunday School in the Star School when the Rev. William Bishop, the Presbyterian minister from Salina, can ride out. I know the Robinsons, Robbs, Lamkins, Ritters and Crawfords have been attending, along with Larry Lapsley, who is at every function at Star School. They plan to build a church in Bridgeport next year.

September 14

Erick and Magdalena had a baby girl today. They named her Hulda Elvira. I believe I am pregnant again.

September 27

Lars Peterson died on the 23rd. Even though he was 71, he hadn't been sick until a few days ago. Lars had been threshing and apparently inhaled too much dust. It paralyzed his lungs and killed him.

We went to the funeral to console Måns and Ola and their families. A gentle rain dampened our shoulders as we stood in the cemetery. I can't say how many times in the past 10 years I have stood in the Assaria graveyard for a funeral. It has been too many.

Today after church we met Lars' brother, Pehr, who must be over 80. He traveled from Sweden to see his sons (the Hesslers) and Lars. He arrived two days after his brother died. They had not seen each other since Lars left Sweden.

October 24

Saturday night is bath night. We pull the tin tub into our bedroom by the stove, heat enough water in the kettle to pour a couple of inches in the tub and start with the youngest child. It is an all-night process by the time eight of us bathe. We need to be clean for church and the older children will attend Luther League tomorrow night. Between church, school and community socials, it seems like we are going somewhere every week. The older the children are, the more activities they want to attend. Last week they went to a taffy pull at neighbor Sven Olson's house.

December 15

The children have asked for autograph books for Christmas. Several children at school have them. The idea is that you have your friends write a poem or verse in your book. When Peter and I were shopping in Lindsborg this week, I bought each child an autograph book from Eberhardt's Bookstore.

1886

Losing a Child

January 7

We have had a terrible blizzard the last two days. The drifts are as high as the eaves on the south side of the barn. The high winds are whipping snow into huge drifts across the road. Peter has strung a line between the house and the barn so he can safely get back and forth. I'm afraid that farmers may lose some livestock if the animals are not in a protected area. The temperature has been below zero for days. This storm is deadly.

To keep the children occupied, we made a large batch of *skorpor.* The smell of the milk-soaked bread, sprinkled with cinnamon and sugar slowly drying in the oven lifted their spirits. Times like these I tell about the winters in Sweden. We had more snow over a longer period of time in Sweden, but not the high winds and snowdrifts like we get in Kansas.

January 17

When Pastor was talking today about "The Lord giveth, and the Lord taketh away," it made me think about recent events. Hannah and Peter Olson added a son, Joseph Cornelius, to their family on the 5th. But while the blizzard raged, our neighbor Emma Lamkin died in childbirth. Charles could not get help because of the storm.

March 7

We have received the new Sears and Roebuck catalog in the mail. The children spend hours looking at the pictures and practicing their English by reading the advertisements. I would love to order a sewing machine. We shall see how wheat harvest goes this year and if we have extra money for such a luxury.

Our church is sponsoring the Kansas Church Conference, March 10-14. It was quite an honor to be selected. The women of the church must fix food for the visiting delegates. I will be spending two days there serving meals.

Peter and Hannah bought the farm straight north of us. Peter missed farming, like I figured he would. He was over to see if we had any milk cows we would want to sell. I have been churning butter and selling it at Bridgeport, so we didn't want to get rid of any cows right now.

March 19

I am drained. This morning I delivered a stillborn baby girl. I have had some pains the last few days, but it got worse last night. Peter wanted to get Dr. Bradley yesterday, but I didn't think it was necessary. I thought I could just take it easy for a few days and I would be all right. The baby came two months early. She was so small, I don't think she would have lived long if she had been breathing.

Peter is building her a tiny casket. I asked that she be buried in Andrew's pasture. I feel like it was my fault that the baby did not live. I let Peter down. He was hoping for a boy to carry on the Runeberg name.

June 2

President Cleveland married Frances Folsom today. He is 49 and she is 21. The newspaper says that the president has known Miss Folsom since she was an infant, and became her court-appointed guardian when her father died 10 years ago. Apparently a different relationship evolved as she got older. They were married at the White House. John Philip Sousa and the Marine band provided the music for the ceremony. The newspaper press is having a field day with this almost scandal from Washington.

July 30

We sat on the porch this evening and enjoyed the summer breeze. The full moon cast shadows around the house. The sky glittered with a million stars and a hundred fireflies. The sound of the frogs and the cicadas blended into the mellow evening. The younger children played hide-and-seek. This is the hour for Peter and I to spend time together and hear about each other's day.

Peter was in Lindsborg today for errands. He saw that Bethany College has started on its first building. He also heard that Pastor LeVeau is leaving our church. Now we must go through the long process of calling another pastor.

September 11

Carrie rode with Peter to Gibson & Thorstenbergs' Lumber Yard in Assaria today. Mr. Thorstenberg has a big cone of hard-pressed sugar and a little hammer on his desk. When children come in with their parents, he chips off a little piece of sugar for them. Needless to say, if Carrie gets a chance to go to town to the lumberyard, she beats Peter to the wagon.

October 4

Broomcorn is becoming a big industry in this area. The New Gottland and Hayes townships have the most broomcorn in the area, but most farmers grow at least a few acres since it is a good cash crop. A broom factory was built in Lindsborg in '80. McPherson has two factories.

Willie is helping the Robinsons with the broomcorn harvest this year. It is a hard job. The stalks, which can be 8 to12 feet tall, must be cut by hand and bundled. The bundles are brought into a shed, where the stalk is scraped until only the straight stalk is left. After that's done, it is loaded into wagons and delivered to the factories.

December 14

The Christmas season has started, but I have not been able to get into the mood of celebrating this year. The approaching birth of Jesus reminds me of my loss this spring.

This morning before breakfast, I made a tiny wreath out of red ribbon and a cedar branch I curled into a circle. After the younger children left for school, I asked Christina to watch Julia for awhile. Seeing the wreath in my hand, she sensed I was going to visit the baby's grave in Andrew's pasture.

Peter, Julia and Kajsa

1887

The Railroad

February 4

Assaria now has a newspaper, *The Assaria Argus*. Now we will be able to keep up on the local news.

There are 63 children enrolled in Star School this year. The parents in the south end of the district have decided to split from Star School and build their own schoolhouse two miles south. They voted on the name Peewee School for the Peewee Creek that flows through that area.

February 24

The Western Railroad Company is building a line through the towns of Gypsum, Bridgeport, Lindsborg and on west. Representatives from our Liberty Township and Smoky View Township met with the representatives of the railroad tonight at Star School to talk about it. The Assaria people were very upset that the train will bypass Assaria and go through Bridgeport instead. Unfortunately, it will go through the north end of our farm. There is nothing we can do about it but take the money that they offered.

March 24

We have a new pastor, just out of seminary at Rock Island, Illinois. Pastor Theodor Kjillgren will be greeted by the 238 members of our congregation next Sunday.

B.G. Gröndal has opened a photography studio in Lindsborg. Peter wanted a picture of us and Julia, so when we were in Lindsborg for supplies this week we had one taken. We saw that the work is progressing on the Brunswick Hotel. It is going to be a three-story red brick structure.

April 4

Peter bought a new fruit from the general store in Assaria today. It is called a banana. It is long and yellow and grows in a huge clump. The clerk told him to peel the yellow skin off and eat the inside. It does not taste like any fruit I've ever eaten.

May 9

The railroad crews have started to work on our land this week. It is quite a process just to get ready for the railroad track. There is the constant noise of the men shouting to the teams, harnesses jingling and overloaded wagons groaning with the weight of the dirt. A bed must be built up to a higher elevation, then railroad ties and rail must be laid. They will also have to build a bridge to get the train across the river. The rhythm of the sledgehammers hitting the spikes has become an everyday sound. Peter and our mule team are working for the railroad too. The soil for the railroad grade is being scraped off of a field from the Lamkin farm to the west of us.

May 20

The rail crews and their teams of horses and mules have camped in our south field while they are working on this length of track. I've told the girls not to go out there without me. I imagine there are a few shady characters in the bunch. Julia is fascinated by the talking around the campfires at night. I'm glad her bedroom window doesn't face south, or I'd never get her to sleep.

I've made a little money by selling bread and pies to the workers. Most of these men are ordinary folk, missing their families and their wives' cooking. They are happy to see me and the girls come out at noon with our baskets full of bread. Julia has been handing out the rolls one by one to the men. They enjoy it when she says, "Here is my biscuit for you." So now they are called "Julia's Biscuits" by the crew

We have also sold produce from our garden. A slice of watermelon tastes pretty good after a long day of toil and sweat.

116

Some neighbors are working for the railroad too, but are close enough to go home at night. The pay is low from the railroad, but it will help buy supplies this winter.

July 11

I lost my black stone pin in the yard yesterday. It was very special to me because Carl gave it to me a month before he died. I didn't realize it was missing until one of the girls commented about it after supper. It was too dark to look, so we waited until this morning to search. It stormed and rained last night and the hogs got out and went through the yard. It is a muddy mess and all torn up. I'm sure the pin got stepped into the mud. We'll keep looking.

September 30

The Assaria Argus had a contest for the largest watermelon in the area. The winner weighed 32 pounds. Alma entered one from our patch but it was only about 20 pounds.

October 31

The train engine chugs by, heading down the grade to the river bridge. Smoke and sparks pour out of the smokestack. The conductor usually waves at us when we are within sight. The train scared us and rattled the livestock for a while, but we've become accustomed to the noise as it goes by, shaking the ground we stand on. The only problem now is we must be on the lookout for fires started by the sparks from the train. More than once we've had to slap wet gunny sacks on an approaching flicker. Peter keeps a firebreak plowed around the farm now.

Our farm has seen a multitude of changes since Carl, Christina and I homesteaded here. We would never have dreamed that a train, like the one we traveled to Kansas in, would chug through our place every day. I guess that is called progress.

December 24

We put up a Christmas tree in the parlor this year. Peter cut a cedar down by the creek. The children strung popcorn and cranberries to put on the tree. Peter surprised me with a box of glass tree ornaments. They are so delicate and fragile.

Peter is treating me like a fragile ornament since I am pregnant again. He is taking good care of me.

Julia's Biscuits

2 cups warm water and milk
1 cake yeast
2 teaspoons salt
1/4 cup sugar
2 cups flour
2 tablespoons lard
Beat good. Add flour (about 2 1/2 to 3 cups) and knead down.
Make little pillows of dough. Let rise, then bake.

1888

Finishing the House

February 27

The Assaria town council has decided to keep out the people from Salina and McPherson because of the smallpox epidemic. We will stay close to home for a while too. Many have died in these towns and I don't want to take any chances. No one in our neighborhood has gotten sick with it yet.

March 27

Mabel Adelaide (named for Adelaide Robinson) was born today. Having a baby at age 43 wasn't as easy as it was 22 years ago when Christina was born. Julia was so happy to get a little sister to play with her. She told the other girls that now she is a "big sister" too.

April 8

Emma and Frank were sponsors for Mabel's baptism today. Julia came up to the baptismal font and watched. She had many questions after the ceremony, asking why Pastor poured water on Mabel's head.

May 1

The children helped me plant a lilac bush on the northeast corner of the house today. Julia wanted to dig the first shovelful and she struggled with it until she got some soil out of the hole. I love the color and smell of lilacs. This plant will give me pleasure every spring as its blossoms burst into perfumed lavender clusters. Even though lilacs bloom here in May, it reminds me of the flowers blooming in Sweden around Midsummer's Day.

May 4

The Assaria Argus reports that 9,000 pounds of milk are arriving daily at the creamery. I didn't realize it was that big an operation. If we have extra milk, we usually take it to the cheese factory in Bridgeport when we go to get the mail.

May 5

Alma was confirmed at the Assaria Church. She did very well on her catechism studies. She has a knack for learning Bible verses. I was extremely proud of her today.

June 6

Theo Pehrson, who lives northwest of Assaria Church, had an accident with the old McCormick binder he was using. The needle pierced right through his forearm when he was reaching for something. He had to use his pocketknife to cut the flesh to get free. I wonder if he will ever use that arm again. I just hate it when the men have to work around those machines.

July 4

We packed a picnic basket and spent the whole day in Assaria for the Independence Day celebration. There was a parade, then a band concert in Hessler's Park, plenty of ice cream to eat and so many people to visit with. The evening was topped off with a fireworks display. Someone said the town council spent $200 for the balloons and fireworks.

The big talk in town though was the drought that seems to be taking its toll on everyone's crops. I think we needed one night of lights and excitement.

July 31

Johan and Eva have decided to sell their land and start over in Minnesota. They have had a hard time this year with the wheat price being so low and they were already deep in debt. Johan had seen advertisements claiming that after a man cleared the land in Minnesota and sold the timber, he had rich soil for farming. The family, including Sven and Katarina, left today on the train for Clarissa, Minnesota.

It was a scant harvest due to the drought. There are several businesses in Assaria that are closing.

August 4

It is so hot in the kitchen during the summer. It seems like we don't get enough air moving in the room some days. We've decided to add a summer kitchen on the west side of the house, just off of the kitchen. When we cook for the harvest crews, it gets unbearably hot, and canning steams up the kitchen all day. We are going to put doors on both the north and south walls of the summer kitchen so the breeze can blow through. It will just be a lean-to on the side of the house, nothing fancy, since it won't be seen from the road, but very practical.

The addition will help keep the cold winds from blowing directly into the kitchen during the winter too. Now there will be a place to store the winter coats and boots while they thaw and drip on the floor. We can build a row of shelves on the west wall for storage. Oh yes, this might be the best room of all!

November 2

Erick died today from pneumonia. He was only 51. Baby Martin is not a month old yet. Magdalena has a hard life ahead of her with three babies so young. I believe her parents will move in to help out with the children and farm chores.

Erick will be buried beside our parents on Sunday. I will miss him so much. I relied on my big brother when Carl died. Now it is my turn to help Magdalena.

December 7

My baby Christina's 22nd birthday. Swan Nelson has asked her to marry him. They have set next February 24 as their wedding date.

December 31

We didn't have the money to finish the house this year but we will get it done eventually. Besides the summer kitchen, we need to rebuild the porches. I want a fancy porch on the east, facing the road, with carved poles and gingerbread trim. We should change the south porch to match the east one and screen it in to keep out the mosquitoes and flies. The north porch will enclose the cistern hole and should be enclosed with screen too.

I want to paint the house a light lemon yellow, with gingerbread trim around the eaves painted in shades of cream, yellow and green. We might not get that done for a year or two, but that is my goal.

Mabel and Julia will never know what our life and farm was like when we first lived here. Whenever I use a bowl or kitchen tool that Carl carved for me, I tell the girls stories about our early days. They can't imagine living in a dugout alone on the vast prairie. Unfortunately, my parents have passed on without the younger girls getting to know them. They could have told so many stories about the Old Country.

I have been in America over 20 years, yet I still get a twinge of longing in my heart for Sweden. But my family is around me and Carl and our lost daughter are buried nearby.

I have come to love my land in America. We worked hard to carve the fields out of the virgin prairie. Now I could not leave this patch of land in the middle of Kansas. This farm will always be home.

The homestead

Glossary

bolagshuset: land company house, the community center
fader: father
frukt soppa: dried fruit cooked into a soup
God Jul: Merry Christmas
Hosianna: name of the Swedish song, "Hosanna"
Julafton: Christmas Eve
Julotta: Early morning Christmas church service
kringler: pastry with sugar icing and nuts
kräm: cooked grape juice sauce
ljus krona: means lighted crown, a Christmas decoration
　　　　　　with candles on the end of the branches
lutfisk: dried stockfish, soaked, then cooked
moder: mother
morfar: maternal grandfather
mormor: maternal grandmother
Nytt och Gammalt: *New and Old,* the name of a newspaper
ostkaka: a custard dessert or cheesecake
pepparkakor: ginger or molasses cookies
potatiskorv: sausage made with ground meat,
　　　　　　onions, potatoes and spices
Psalmbok: Psalm Book
risan pudding: cooked rice pudding
sillsallad: salad made with herring, beets and potatoes
skorpor: rusks, dried bread with cinnamon and sugar
smörbakelser: butter cookies
smörgåsbord: variety of foods served buffet style
Svenska Härolden: *The Swedish Herald,* a newspaper
svärfar: father-in-law
svärmor: mother-in-law
tack så mycket: thank you very much

MARRIAGE LICENSE.

SALINE COUNTY, STATE OF KANSAS,
December 19"" A. D. 1883.

TO ANY PERSON AUTHORIZED BY LAW TO PERFORM THE MARRIAGE CEREMONY:

Greeting: You are hereby authorized to join in Marriage *Peter Runeberg* of *Bridgeport Kansas* aged _29_ years, and *Mrs. Mary C. Swanson* of *Bridgeport Kansas* aged _39_ years, and of this License you will make due return to my office within thirty days.

Jonathan Weaver
Probate Judge.

STATE OF KANSAS, } ss.
SALINE COUNTY.

I _____ do hereby certify that in accordance with the authorization of the within License, I did, on _____ day of _____ A. D., 1883__, at _____ in said County, join and unite in marriage the within named *Peter Runeberg* and *Mary C. Swanson*

Witness my Hand and Seal this day and year above written.

_____
_____

Attest *Jonathan Weaver* _____ *Probate Judge.*

Marriage License of Peter and Kajsa Runeberg

Bibliography

PUBLISHED MATERIAL

40th Anniversary Album of the Evangelical Lutheran Congregation of Salemsborg, 1869-1959.

100th Anniversary Yearbook, Bethany Lutheran Church, Lindsborg, Kansas. Wichita, KS: Jeffery's of Kansas, 1969.

Alderson, Nanie T., and Smith, H.H. *A Bride Goes West.* Farrar and Rinehart, Inc., 1942. Lincoln, NE: University of Nebraska Press, Second Bison Book printing, 1969.

Assaria, Kansas, 80th Anniversary, 1886-1966.

Beard, Charles A. *The Presidents in American History.* New York: Julia Messner, 1969.

Billdt, Ruth. *Pioneer Swedish-American Culture in Central Kansas.* Lindsborg, KS: Lindsborg News-Record, 1965.

Billdt, Ruth, and Jaderborg, Elizabeth. *The Smoky Valley in the After Years.* Lindsborg, KS: Lindsborg News-Record, 1969.

Bokförlaget Prisma. *Prisma's English-Swedish Dictionary.* Minneapolis: University of Minnesota Press, 1988.

Bokförlaget Prisma. *Prisma's Swedish-English Dictionary.* Minneapolis: University of Minnesota Press, 1988.

Broadfoot, Barry. *The Pioneer Years, 1895-1914.* Toronto: Doubleday Canada Limited, 1976.

Dahl, K.G. Wm. *Children of the Prairie.* Dr. Sam Dahl and Miriam Dahl Lindgren, Publishers, 1984.

Deaths and Interments- Salina Co., Kansas 1859-1985. Compiled by the Smoky Valley Genealogical Society and Library Inc., 1985.

DeGregorio, William A. *The Complete Book of U.S. Presidents.* New York: Dembner Books, 1984.

Farnsworth, Martha. *Plains Woman—The Diary of Martha Farnsworth, 1882-1922.* Bloomington, IN: Indiana University Press, 1985.

Gabrielson, Clarence Wesley. *Far Far Dagar.* Wichita, KS: Wichita High School Heights Printing Class, 1979.

Gunby, Lise. *Early Farm Life.* New York: Crabtree Publishers, 1983.

Kalman, Bobbie. *The Early Family Home.* New York: Crabtree Publishers, 1982.

Kalman, Bobbie. *Food for the Settler.* New York: Crabtree Publishers, 1982.

Levenson, Dorothy. *Women of the West.* New York: Watts, 1973.

Lind, Selma. [Jaderborg, E.] *Marmeluke Rambo Ericksson.* McPherson, KS: Modern Graphics, 1969.

Lindquist, Emory. *The Smoky Valley People: A History of Lindsborg, Kansas.* Rock Island, IL: Augustana Book Concern, 1953.

Lindsborg Efter Femtio År. Rock Island, IL: Augustana Book Concern, 1919.

Lindsborg pa Svensk-Amerikansk Kulturbild från Mellersta Kansas. Rock Island, IL: Augustana Book Concern, 1909.

Miner, Craig. West of Wichita: Settling the High Plains of Kansas, 1865-1890. Lawrence, KS: University Press of Kansas, 1986.

Minnes Album—Svenska Lutherska Församlingen, Salemsborg, Kansas, 1869-1909. Rock Island, IL: Augustana Book Concern, 1909.

Moberg, Vilhelm. *The Emigrants.* New York: Warner Books/ Simon and Schuster, 1983.

Moberg, Vilhelm. *The Last Letter Home*. New York: Simon and Schuster, 1961.

Moberg, Vilhelm. *The Settlers*. New York: Popular Library, 1978.

Moberg, Vilhelm. *Unto a Good Land*. New York: Simon and Schuster, 1954.

My Folks Came in a Covered Wagon. Edited by Louise Fowler Roote and Alta Maxwell Huff. Stauffer Communications, Inc., 1956.

My Folks Claimed the Plains. Edited by Virginia Haggart and Dorothy Harvey. Stauffer Communications, Inc., 1978.

Myres, Sandra L. *Westering Women and the Frontier Experience, 1800-1915*. Albuquerque: University of New Mexico Press, 1982.

Odin Ltd. *Mormor's Immigrant Cookbook—1897*. Lindsborg, KS: Carlson's Publishing, 1991.

Olsson, Anna. *A Child of the Prairie*. Translated by Martha Winblad, edited by Elizabeth Jaderborg, 1978.

Pihl, Johan Augustin. *God's People in a New Land*. Edited by Vernon C.F. Holm. Lindsborg, KS: Smoky Valley Historical Publications, 1984.

Riley, Glenda. *The Female Frontier*. Lawrence, KS: University Press of Kansas, 1988.

Ruede, Howard. *Sod-House Days: Letters from a Kansas Homesteader, 1877-78*. Edited by John Ise. Lawrence, KS: University Press of Kansas, 1983.

Schlissel, Lillian. *Women's Diaries of the Westward Journey*. New York: Schocken Books, 1981.

Seed for the Harvest, The Trojan, Vol. IX. 1975-76. Southeast of Saline Senior High School, 1976.

Seventy-Fifth Anniversary 1875-1950, Assaria Lutheran Church, Assaria, Kansas. Topeka, KS: Myers and Co., 1950.

Stratton, Joanna L. *Pioneer Women—Voice From the Kansas Frontier*. New York: Simon and Schuster, 1981.

Superbly Swedish. Edited by Martha Wiberg Thompson. Iowa City, IA: Penfield Press, 1983.

Todd, Verna Perrill. *Bridgeport Church and Community.* 1962.

U.S. Government records.

Vid Fyrtioårsfesten, Svenska Evangeliskt Lutherska Assaria Församlingen i Assaria, Kansas Den 6-8 Okt. 1916.

Woodward, Mary Dodge. *The Checkered Years: A Bonanza Farm Diary—1884-88.* Edited by Mary Boynton Cowdrey. St. Paul, MN: Minnesota Historical Society Press, 1989.

UNPUBLISHED MATERIAL

"Assaria Forty-Year Celebration."

"Assaria Lutheran Church records."

Bloomberg, Emelia. "Dates of the Family."

Hoglund, Melvina. "Bloomberg Cemetery."

Johnson, Linda. "The Early History of Assaria, Kansas."

Learned, Lily. "The History of Larry Lapsley."

Olson, Julia. "A Bit of History for My Children and Their Children."

Peterson, Alma. "History of Lone Star School."

Peterson, Hulda Johnson. "Our Dad and Mother."

Peterson, O.L. "The Family Line of Lars Pehron."

Redden, L. "Memories of the Ola Lars Peterson Family."

Redden, Laurina. "Hallville, My Home Town."

Schaeffer, Rozella. "Peter Olson—Hannah Carlson Olson."

Schaeffer, Rozella. "Peter and Hannah Olson."

"Salemsborg Lutheran Church records."

Swenson, Karl J. "Swenson Family Tree."